EDGAR CAYCE'S GUIDE
TO SPIRITUALITY
FOR BUSY PEOPLE

Other Books by Mark Thurston

EDGAR CAYCE'S GUIDE TO SPIRITUALITY FOR BUSY PEOPLE

by Mark Thurston, Ph.D.

ASSOCIATION FOR RESEARCH AND ENLIGHTENMENT

A.R.E. Press   •   Virginia Beach   •   Virginia

A.R.E. Press
215 67th Street
Virginia Beach, VA 23451-2061

The three main sections of this book were formerly published
by A.R.E. Press as booklets under the titles of *Attain Peace and
Surrender Fear, Free Yourself to Love Unconditionally,* and *Slow
Down and Simplify Your Life* © 1991 by the Edgar Cayce Foundation.

Thurston, Mark A.
    Edgar Cayce's guide to spirituality for busy people / by Mark
Thurston.
        p.   cm.
    ISBN 0-87604-467-4 (pbk.)
    1. Spiritual life. 2. Cayce, Edgar, 1877-1945. I. Title: Guide to
spirituality for busy people. II. Title.
BL624.T472   2000
291.4'4—dc21

                                                    99-089267

Edgar Cayce Readings © 1971, 1993, 1994, 1995, 1996
by the Edgar Cayce Foundation. All rights reserved.

Cover design by Lightbourne

Contents

Part Three: Free Yourself to Love Unconditionally

Foreword

Edgar Cayce is America's best-documented clairvoyant and spiritual philosopher. Over a period of forty-three years during the first half of the twentieth century, he gave over 14,000 psychic discourses for people who needed help. The material addressed all the basic themes of human experience.

Fortunately, the counsel that he offered was recorded and is still available to us today. His messages are every bit as relevant, timely, and applicable today as they were when he gave them.

This book offers vital help to readers on three important themes that can facilitate happier, healthier lives: how to slow down and live at a more healthful pace, how to surrender fear and create peace in your life, and how to engender unconditional love in the way you live.

Each brief chapter begins with a quote taken from one of Cayce's readings. (The numeric notations after each short passage indicates an indexing number within the collection of this work, used to protect the identity of the person who received the reading.)

Following the quotes are commentaries, some of which elaborate on Cayce's central ideas, while others tell the fascinating story of the person who received the advice from Cayce. (Fictitious names are used to preserve anonymity.) All these commentaries are designed to inspire you and to suggest ways to begin using the principles to improve your life through spiritual growth.

Finally, each chapter concludes with a clear statement of how you can apply and live that principle. Each of these "mini-motivators" is designed to get you focused and moving toward an *application* of a life-changing principle.

Take your time going through this book. Spend a day—or sometimes several days—thinking about and applying the ideas. Find the ones that work best for you. By following that simple formula, and *acting* on the ideas, you will achieve the best results.

So let's get started. Only two things are required of you as we begin. First, you need to have recognized your own *sincere desire* to change the quality of how you're living your life. Second, you should feel a *willingness to experiment* with some changes. The results you'll get from this book may surprise you.

PART ONE

SLOW DOWN AND SIMPLIFY YOUR LIFE

Be not impatient with thine brother, with thine neighbor, and—most of all—with thine self.

Edgar Cayce Reading 262-44

Introduction

The pace of modern life can sometimes overwhelm us. We hasten from one appointment to another. We clutter up our weekly schedules, hardly leaving room for what we really enjoy. Hoping to fit everything in, we look for time-saving shortcuts: fast foods, express lines, news summaries.

It's a sad fact of contemporary life that impatience is the norm. All too often we feel as if someone or something is trying to hurry us. We get caught up in the tyranny of clock time. And then, whether or not we mean to, we can easily slip into rushing other people: we become the ones hurrying them along.

We need to learn how to slow down, to pay more attention to the quality of our lives and not just the quantity of what we've accomplished. We'd better get started in this direction because, if anything, the years ahead are likely to be filled with even *more* temptation to speed anxiously through life.

Learning how to slow down and simplify your life may not be as hard as you think. Of course, it takes a real desire and determination to initiate some changes. But once you've made a commitment to yourself, the steps are straightforward and within reach.

Vitality

(Q) Why am I so tense?
(A) For you are so alive! But leave self more and more in that attitude of *resting* in Him. Tenseness here, for this entity, bespeaks the vitality, the desire to be *doing!* Hence the warning—in thy doing, do not become too material-minded.   2403-1

THERE'S so much to get excited about in today's world. In spite of all the problems, it's a fantastic opportunity to be alive now. Compared to other times in human history, we have so many choices and diverse options. But some-times all those alternatives lead to tension. We have to wade through countless facts and figures as we weigh competing possibilities. And then we worry whether or not we've made the right choices. That's the sort of situa-tion in which one woman found herself and turned to Edgar Cayce for advice.

"Why am I so tense?" That's the question that tormented Eileen. Everyone knew her as a live wire, full of ideas and action. But those who knew her best saw something else; an undercurrent of tension. She recognized it, too, and was concerned that something might be seriously wrong in her character. So when she got a reading from Cayce, this was one of the questions she wanted answered.

Eileen may have been surprised, because his answer started out on such a positive note. It can be your very aliveness that indirectly leads to tension. Tension can easily go with being in a world that is full of possibilities.

In fact, tension has been labeled an unquestionable villain in our times. We constantly hear of maladies such as tension headaches and tension-produced illnesses. No doubt, tension can have those detrimental effects. But maybe the place to start dealing with it is our very attitude and belief. Sometimes tension is simply a byproduct of our "vitality, the desire to be *doing!*"

Maybe that vital, creative energy needs to be channeled in a more balanced way. Or maybe our desires ought to be tempered because we can't do everything at once. But in our need to be less tense, let's remember to be appreciative of our choices and opportunities. Most of us wouldn't trade places with people who lived 300 years ago at a time when life was less tense, but the possibilities were a lot more limited.

Mini-motivator: When you wake up in the morning— before your mind becomes preoccupied with everything to do that day—take a moment to feel and appreciate your own vitality and the many wonderful opportunities life offers to you.

Easing Up

Do not *try* too hard, for when we try hard we become too conscious of self—and it is selflessness [that] we are to attain . . . Be *joyous* in thy love of others, as of thy Maker.
3051-2

$STOP$ pressing. You're only making it hard on yourself. Ease up.

Have you ever gotten those kinds of suggestions when things weren't going well? The friend who offered that advice saw a problem that's often involved in achieving goals: sometimes you can be your own worst enemy.

It's a curious paradox. Anything worth having in life requires desire and effort; a good job, solid relationships, steady health. They all demand work.

But unfortunately, the very qualities that start us toward our goals can turn against us if they're overdone. When effort becomes strain, we're in trouble. When desire becomes compulsion, we're going to get frustrated.

What happens when you try too hard? Whether you intend it or not, it's a *power play.* Pressing for what you want makes an indirect statement: "*I* am the sole source of power and influence in my life. I am the cause—my goal is the effect."

On the one hand, that sort of attitude seems admi-

4

rable. It sounds like a willingness to take personal responsibility. Who can argue with that? But beneath the surface, such an attitude is flawed because of what it leaves out. Seeing yourself as the exclusive force that shapes your life is what Cayce called becoming "too conscious of self."

Trusting in a higher power is the missing ingredient whenever you make a power play. Having faith in God—that's what's forgotten when desire turns into compulsion, when effort shifts gears and becomes strain. Or, put another way, when you're trying too hard, you're not really loving the Creator. When you act as if it's totally up to you and you alone, then the creative flow is interrupted. No wonder things stop working. It should be no surprise that straining and stretching is bound to block success.

So, what's the answer? This simple secret: Be joyous in the love of your Maker. Celebrate the fact that you've got an extraordinary Ally. For every effort toward your goal that reflects love and creativity, you're actually a *co*creator. There's no need to strain, so you can ease up. If a project or goal is really right—for you and everyone else—it's going to be successful. Just do your part, nothing more.

What a relief! What a joy when you simplify your life and resist the temptation to force matters. You can trust the Creator to be a Partner in all your dreams.

Mini-motivator: Pick a situation in your life that's not going as well as you'd like—one in which you catch yourself straining to make things work the way you'd like. Try easing up. Be willing to do your part to make things work out, but leave room for a higher force to play its role.

Everything Is Purposeful

Do not make haste other than slowly in gaining the perfect understanding of the purpose of life in this mundane sphere; for while it should be the *ideal* of every individual to succeed . . . fame and fortune often take wings unless same are the *result* and not the *end* of a life spent in understanding what life's all about!   5616-1

WILLIAM was in trouble—financial trouble. His personal debt was piling up and there was no way he could get his head above water if he relied on his weekly paycheck alone. His life was now caught up in a desperate attempt to satisfy his creditors. The stress was taking a toll on his health and his relationships: high blood pressure, insomnia, nervous tension, and marital problems.

He urgently contacted Edgar Cayce for advice. Maybe a clairvoyant could see a way out of this stressful maze. Even though he had never before sought information from Cayce, it seemed as if this source would be his last resort.

"Will my personal financial situation improve—when—how can I quickly lessen within reason the load of personal debts—should I try to make money outside of . . . Co.? If so, how?"

Soon the reading came. It was straightforward and

hopeful. The advice was simple: Don't panic. Don't hurry. Don't indulge in worrisome speculation.

Success—real success—is a byproduct, not an end in itself. Even though it's natural to want to get back on top of things financially, you'd better be sure you go about this right or you'll only dig yourself into a deeper hole.

Every day little opportunities arise which can be part of the solution. If your life is in a fearful tizzy, you're not going to recognize them, or you're going to settle for options that don't really measure up to your highest values.

So first, slow down. Relax. Settle in for the long haul. Things are going to get better if you patiently remember that the purpose of life is to *understand.* Try to be around people who help you better understand yourself and life. When you've got a choice about where to put your professional energies, pick the alternative that appears to be supportive of that ideal.

Finally, trust that your life has a plan. With clairvoyance it can be seen that important opportunities are coming your way. Within the next two months, a situation will come up and give you the chance to get ahead financially. Watch for it and be ready to act. But even more important—even if you hadn't gotten this psychic counsel about your future—remember that the best advice is always to take life slowly, carefully, and with deep trust that everything happens for a purpose.

That was good advice for William in 1929—a year of great troubles. It's just as sound and reliable for us today.

Mini-motivator: Respond to a hard, difficult day in a new way. Instead of worrying or trying to hurry matters to change, adopt an attitude of *trust.* Slow down. Believe that events are happening for a purpose.

Being Kind

Not in some great deed of heroism; not in some great speech or act that may be pointed to with pride—but rather in the little kindnesses from day to day . . .   3795-1

THE harsh words just slipped out. As soon as he said them, he knew it wasn't right. But he was impatient and just blurted out what he was feeling at that moment.

How often has that happened to you? How often has your impatience or your hectic lifestyle spilled over into unkindness with other people? It happens at least occasionally to virtually everyone. Perhaps the best remedy is to remember just how important kindness really is— how much people need kindness and how deeply they're affected by it.

A society that's in a hurry is sure to be short on one commodity: kindness. We tend to be so self-concerned, so stressed out with our own agendas that we forget to really care about the feelings of others. But accepting blame and feeling guilty about it doesn't make us any more likely to be kind the next time. If anything, guilt only makes us feel resentful that we're expected to be kind—it becomes yet another obligation added to our list of burdens.

Maybe we can find a stimulus to greater kindness in a

quite unexpected place. Rather than fight head-on the values and priorities of our busy, ambitious world, let's try turning around one of its basic principles. For example, a guiding rule of our commercial, technological culture is to take advantage of "leverage" whenever one can. Leverage simply means getting a big impact out of a small effort. Financiers use it by borrowing huge sums of money for their transactions, hoping to make a big profit without having to use very much of their own money.

But what might be a way of utilizing the principle of leverage in the spiritual realm? Where might relatively small investments of time, energy, or effort result in big steps for soul growth? In our dealings with others, the answer is sure to be *kindness.*

The clearest way to recognize this fact is to remember times when you were on the receiving end of kindness. How did it make you feel when a busy supervisor stopped in the middle of her frantic schedule and sincerely thanked you for a job well done? What went on inside you when a family member noticed that you weren't feeling well and gladly picked up the slack for you? What happened to your self-esteem when a new acquaintance called you by your name the next time you met?

Probably what you've felt whenever you've been on the receiving end of kindness is simply this: a desire and willingness *to recommit even more of yourself* to the job, the family, or the relationship. Kindness has an extraordinary power that calls forth the best in people. What makes it so magical is how little it takes to get huge results.

In other words, it's just plain *smart* to be kind. There's no need to moralize with yourself about it. You don't have to back in to being kind because you're trying to avoid feeling guilty. It simply makes a lot of sense to invest small amounts of genuine concern in the way you meet people day by day.

Mini-motivator: Be smart today—spiritually smart, that is. Take time to be kind. With just a few words or with small deeds, take time to show others how much you genuinely care about them.

Slowly Doing Your Best

Make haste slowly. Be not overanxious. Be intense, yes. Be
consistent, sure. Be ye perfect, yes—even as ye desire that
others be. But leave much of the results with Him . . .

2441-2

"MAKE haste slowly." This was one of Edgar Cayce's
most frequent pieces of advice to those busy, stressed
people who received readings. At first glance the words
appear contradictory, paradoxical. Cayce's suggestion
seems to refute itself. How can anyone be in haste and
also proceed slowly?

Maybe the wisdom in this counsel cannot be understood unless we reconsider what's meant by haste. Nor-
mally we think of synonyms like "hurry," "rush," and
"speed." They all give us a picture of life in the fast lane—
a preoccupation with quickness over quality, with time-
saving over long-term effect. "Haste makes waste," the
old proverb reminds us.

But maybe haste can have another connotation, if it's
coupled with the right spirit. Instead of waste, there's the
potential for efficiency of movement or action: doing
things the *right* way. Another ancient proverb—much
less quoted—states: "The more haste, the less speed."

This latter saying seems to be the meaning at what the

Cayce readings were hinting. Slowing down doesn't necessarily mean surrendering your best intentions and goals. "Make haste slowly." Be efficient in moving toward your ideals. Hold on to your intense desires, your consistent efforts, and your ideals of perfection. But recognize an alternative way of understanding haste. It focuses on efficiency, which means going at a slower speed *and* trusting that higher forces are also at work to assist you.

Mini-motivator: What do you really care about? Where in your life do you feel an intensity and drive to consistently do your best? Hold on to that caring, that commitment—but act slowly and with the spirit of trust that things are unfolding in the best way.

Overcoming Anxiety with Inspiration

Do not work self into a state of overanxiety at the changes
that will be found, or attempt to use up the strength and
vitality . . . Forget not the sources of thine inspiration . . .

480-11

CHANGE is all around us. If anything, the rate of change
will only continue to accelerate in the years ahead. We
need to become better and better at dealing with it.

Of course, it's one thing to handle abstract changes
that don't seem to immediately affect us. Much of what
we read about in magazines or see on the evening news
is just an interesting curiosity. It may irritate us or make
us feel nostalgic, but it appears for the moment to be
rather remote.

But when change hits close to home, it's another matter. Unfortunately, the most natural and automatic reactions only make situations more difficult: anger, resistance,
self-pity. What we really need is a "First Aid Kit for
Change": a small array of methods we could apply on
ourselves whenever changing times hit close to home.

The first item in that kit might well be an antidote to
the strength-depleting effects of change. A person who
is going through a major transition often looks fatigued
and worn out—and there's a good reason why. This indi-

vidual is probably spending considerable time and energy *resisting the adjustment.* He or she may have been temporarily *living a dual life:* keeping the old situation going until it finally winds down, while at the same time trying to get the new elements of life started. That sort of double duty is bound to sap strength.

But the counsel Cayce gave to Sue—who had asked for advice concerning her "own welfare"—points to another significant way that change can rob us of vitality: extreme anxiety. It's something we do to ourselves, that we "work ourselves into." Maybe a little anxiety is natural and unavoidable. We're only human; and when big changes come, some degree of concern is normal. But Cayce's implication is that overanxiety is avoidable. We can catch ourselves before it builds to that debilitating point. We can stop that vicious circle in its tracks. The best way to do that is to turn your mind to something that inspires you. Inspiration will renew you and revitalize you in times of change.

Mini-motivator: The next time you catch yourself becoming overly anxious about changes, turn your mind for a few minutes to something that inspires you. It might be an uplifting piece of music or a special passage from a book. It could be a place to revisit or a few minutes with a person who lifts your spirits.

Setting Realistic Goals

Remember that overenthusiasm is as bad as dilatory activity. Great movements, great forces, move slowly. 1151-21

LAZINESS gets us into lots of trouble. When we put off doing what we know needs to be done, it creates all kinds of problems. Of course, there's a time and place once in a while for "taking it easy," since we all need periodic rejuvenation. But "dilatory activity"—that is, procrastinating, indolent behavior—is a vexing fault.

If laziness is such a shortcoming, what's the compensatory *virtue?* Is it boundless overenthusiasm? Is it a determination to accomplish great things in a very short time? Unfortunately, it's common to make that assumption. But when we try to fight against a lackadaisical nature, we can often end up at the other extreme.

Swinging from one extreme to its opposite is a familiar tendency. In this case, we may see ourselves switching back and forth between two ineffectual habits—as demonstrated by the extremities of the hare in his fabled race with the tortoise. We may oscillate between lazy inactivity and a wild burst of super efforts. But it's in the slow but consistent approach that great things emerge.

One of the clearest ways that overenthusiasm expresses itself is in our grand intentions—plans that contain both a time element *and* a commitment to certain deeds. Out of impulsive spurts of energy we may announce wonderful goals and set a time limit on their completion. "By five o'clock this afternoon I'll have the first chapter written on that term paper I've been avoiding." Or "In the next two hours I'm going to write six overdue letters."

But what have we done in these bursts of overenthusiastic intentions? We've put unnecessary pressure on ourselves. We've boxed ourselves in, and this condition is almost sure to lead to impatient, unsatisfying efforts. The alternative is to use that enthusiasm to commit to either what will get done or how much time will be spent on the activity. "I'm going to work until five o'clock on my term paper, and we'll see how much I can get done." Or "I'm going to get those six overdue letters written, but I don't know how long it's going to take." That's the middle way, an approach that uses the spark of enthusiasm and patiently works with quality effort.

Mini-motivator: The next time you feel a rush of enthusiasm about doing something, carefully formulate your intention. So as not to slide into unrealistic overenthusiasm, limit the scope of your goal. Either commit to a certain amount of time on your project (without a preconceived notion of how much will get done) or commit to a quality task of getting a project finished (without a time limit).

Respecting Your Body

Prepare the body. Prepare the mind, before ye attempt to
loosen it . . .   2475-1

SOME days we'd just like to get away from it all—loosen
all the ties that bind us. Responsibilities, expectations,
and duties seem like too much. It's a time when our
minds may turn to spiritual things. There must be a freer
world, we imagine—a place where we can get loose from
the burdens of material life.

But spirituality seen as an escape is really an illusion.
We're sure to be disappointed if we're running away from
our bodies and their demands, or if we're trying to avoid
memories and feelings that haunt us. To imagine the
spiritual world as a place "to get away from it all" is to
deceive ourselves.

The advice given by Cayce to James is a good reminder
to all of us. James certainly had reason to want to escape.
The tensions and responsibilities he faced were sometimes overwhelming. So he had turned to yoga, both as
a stress-reducer and as a way he could achieve spiritual
experiences. He wanted to get free from his physical
body and his accustomed mental state. He was in a
hurry to make a breakthrough into the spiritual world.

What was wrong with his attitude? What's wrong with

our own whenever we start dreaming of "leaving it all behind"? The fundamental mistake is the belief that there are two quite different worlds: the familiar, physical dimension and a mysterious, ethereal realm of spirit. Actually, it's all one. In truth, the spiritual world is all about us—penetrating matter, permeating every form of life. We may not recognize it, but it's there. Sure, it's possible to have an out-of-body experience or to suddenly find your consciousness in another dimension of awareness. But those experiences are most meaningful and helpful when they come *as a result* of a healthy body and mind, not as an escape from problems.

So what's the answer to our genuine need to know if there is more to life than paying bills and coping with aches and pains? Prepare the body. Prepare the mind. Instead of trying to shake free from your familiar life situation—no matter how tense or how difficult it is—let something *come to you.* Make your body and mind a place where spiritual forces can come alive more freely.

Mini-motivator: Do something today with your body—*for* your body—that will make it more receptive to spiritual forces. It may be a small diet change, an extra period of rest and rejuvenation, or a much-needed exercise time.

Allowing Time for Growth

(Q) What should be my procedure to hasten my spiritual and mental development?
(A) Make haste here slowly. For, this—the spiritual and mental—is as a growth. Ye *grow* in grace, in knowledge, in understanding. And as the application is made daily in thy relationships to others, so is the growth accomplished.

510-2

A secret to inner development is understanding the nature of *growth*. It's easy to take this word for granted, with thinking that goes like this: Growth simply means getting bigger. It's a measure of quantity. The more knowledge I accumulate about spiritual matters, the greater is my spiritual growth. The more meditation sessions I log and the more of my dreams I interpret, the greater is my inner development.

But that way of looking at growth misses something: the *quality* of your experience. Growth reorganizes your understanding; it transforms the way you see yourself and the world around you.

This "other side" of growth is emphasized in a case from the Cayce files. In 1941 an ambitious twenty-five-year-old woman named Beth wrote to Edgar Cayce requesting advice on her vocation. She was a dressmaker and wanted to expand her business. She had identified two options: renovate her garage into a dress shop or rent a storefront in a business district. She hoped that psychic input on this question would lead to the best results.

Rather than answer Beth's question directly, Cayce told her to slow down. Don't proceed too quickly. There's still work for you to do in becoming more and more qualified to own and run a dressmaking business, he told her. By your undertaking of professional growth and development, the question of how to expand might start looking very different. Options other than just those two choices are likely to emerge. Only by moving deliberately and purposefully—without any sense of anxious hurry— will you grow and be able to make the best decision.

In fact, the Cayce readings often linked growth to truth itself. "Truth is a growing thing." This doesn't mean that truth is inconsistent and changing. Instead, it reminds us that as we grow and develop, certain truths become relatively more significant to us. For example, think back and remember which principles or truths were most important to you five years ago. No doubt, they're just as valid today, but different principles may now be more significant to the challenges you're facing. Growth changes the way you understand the situations in your life.

Mini-motivator: Pick a circumstance in your life right now where you feel compelled to make a decision very soon. Slow down and give yourself three more days before making that choice. During that time be especially alert for additional knowledge and understanding. Be prepared for new options that may occur to you.

Imaginary Self-Images

(Q) *Please advise cause and correction of my impression of constant effort to escape and need of great haste — and from what?*
(A) Self. It is the haste from self.   3357-2

HAVE you ever felt the way Mary did? With great honesty she admitted that she often felt as if she were in a hurry and running away from something. But from what? Edgar Cayce's answer was short and to the point: yourself.

The self mentioned here is not the higher self—not the individuality which is the identity of the soul. Instead, this comment refers to the personality, the familiar sense of identity that we live with throughout most of the day. Unfortunately, this side of ourselves has lots of misconceptions. Our personality selves carry false, imaginary notions of who we are. And when we try to live up to those images, we're usually tense and hurried. We run from one demand to another, trying to keep up with a counterfeit picture of ourselves.

We all struggle with our personality selves, so don't feel guilty or alone if you discover how true this is of you. We all have illusions about ourselves. Some are grandiose fantasies of our own importance—what the readings call "self-aggrandizement." Other illusions are harshly low self-appraisals—what the readings call "self-condemnation." It's natural to wonder from where those illusions originate. Some, no doubt, are the result of childhood experiences—or, going even further back, patterns from earlier lives. Some of the false images come from the society in which we live. Others are certainly the product of choices that we've made—decisions to see ourselves in a particular way that may not have been very accurate.

How does your personality operate when it attempts to maintain its hold on you? Trying to keep everyone pleased and struggling to maintain a good impression are two common methods of the personality. They're analogous to constantly standing on your tiptoes. Try to picture what it would be like to stand on your toes for ten minutes . . . or for an hour. What strain and exhaustion come from attempting to conform to imaginary ideas of who you are! No wonder you sometimes find it hard to relax!

To see and admit this fact is a bitter pill. We'd rather see our busy lives as efforts to accomplish lofty goals. But on closer examination, we'll probably see what Mary recognized before turning to Cayce for counsel: tension and hurry are warning signs that something is seriously out of whack.

Mini-motivator: Stop listening so intently to the little voices that drive you. Be willing to surrender your expectations about how every single event is going to turn out. Don't worry if you're not always appreciated, understood, or liked—just so long as you know you're doing what's right. In summary, try for just one day to get off your tiptoes!

Staying Within Yourself

(Q) How can I speed up results in the work?
(A) The results as attained, the service as rendered, must be that to enable the entity to make haste slowly. Do not get ahead of the *good* that is rendered, else we will find . . . confusions arising oft. 967-1

IN your rush to accomplish the tasks of life, you can sometimes get ahead of yourself. This isn't just a figure of speech; it's something you can intuitively feel with your body. There's a distinct sensation that comes from straining beyond the present moment and your available capacities.

Athletes refer to this phenomenon. They know that in order to get their optimum performance they have to "stay within themselves." If they stretch themselves too far, they lose control of their movements. If they try vainly to get ahead of themselves, their performance quickly diminishes.

The same principle holds true for any endeavor. Impatient and anxious behavior is often counterproductive. It frequently creates confusion for yourself and for those around you.

The best approach is to let your efforts bear fruit before trying to move ahead. Allow the positive impact of what's just been done to consolidate and form a solid foundation before moving on to the next step. If you rush ahead too quickly, you're likely to encounter disorder as well as obstacles.

Two images from childhood are good metaphors to illustrate this principle. Perhaps you can remember assembling a wooden or plastic model when you were young. A certain type of glue was required. Once you connected and glued together a few of the pieces, it always needed time to dry and set before you could proceed. If you tried to push ahead too quickly with the task of adding more pieces, you quickly made a mess. The good work you had done at one step had to be given time to consolidate before you could move on.

Another image comes from learning mathematics. When you were in second and third grades, you were probably engaged in studying multiplication tables. If you picked up the algebra textbook of an older brother or sister, the content of those pages might well have frightened you. Strange symbols—letters in place of numbers! What did it all mean? Getting beyond yourself in that way was bound to be a confusing experience. But with time and patience, as your knowledge of basic mathematics was given the opportunity to consolidate itself, then by high school years that algebra book probably didn't look nearly so intimidating.

Mini-motivator: Live this day within yourself. Stop straining and stretching to reach imaginary goals that are currently beyond your capacities. Affirm that those goals may some day be readily attainable. But for today you'll stick with the learning and growth opportunities that are here and now.

Making Little Differences

... proceed slowly, for it is line upon line, precept upon precept, here a little, there a little, until the whole leaven be leavened ...   3976-7

CAYCE was fond of using this homey metaphor of the small bit of leavening that can make all the dough rise for bread-baking. It creates a simple, powerful picture: big results can come from small things. But it's hard to imagine how little things can have the biggest influence. This is surely one of the deepest spiritual mysteries.

Our modern technological world teaches the opposite: If you want to make a big splash, then do something sensational. But this leads to frantic competition with other people. How much of our busy-ness comes from a drive to be noticed and feel important? There's room for only a few at the top of an organization's hierarchy. There's only limited space in the daily newspaper for reports of great happenings, and only so much time on the evening news for stories about what's supposedly important. Must we be self-promoters if we dream of doing something valuable in today's world?

Maybe there's another route—one that doesn't require becoming famous, getting our thoughts published, or appearing on a news program. In the smaller circle of situations in which we find ourselves, the most valuable kind of work can take place. Pain may be eased by a kind word, discouragement erased by a smile, fear dispelled by a courageous deed. Each small event can be seen as a cosmic occurrence.

One way of describing this view of life is "the macrocosm in the microcosm." This simply means that the universal can be found in the specific—that the ultimate can be discovered in the mundane. Life takes on a magical quality when we remember this. Every encounter with someone or something becomes special.

It's this very principle that shaped the dream of a man who was about to be promoted to a prominent position in a high-profile company. He had aspired to this job for many years and had worked hard for it. He knew that it was going to give him a chance to implement some of his ideas. He would start making a difference in his company and in the world.

But then a dream came to change his mind. In the dream he saw himself as a humble servant. His job was to serve food behind a cafeteria line. Surprisingly, he wasn't humiliated by this level of work, because in the dream he was greatly enjoying this way of helping people. Upon awakening, the man quickly recognized the message: You've always had the opportunity to make a difference in the world—it hasn't depended on any promotion at work.

Mini-motivator: Look for some small—but still very significant—difference that you can make in someone's life today. For example, compliment someone, lift a discouraged person's spirits by taking time to care and listen, or write a short letter and make someone feel special.

Oneness Through Suffering

(Q) Give the body any advice as to her future outlook and conduct in all phases of her life, that will be helpful to her.
(A) Be not too hasty. Be long-suffering. Think not of self. Think of others first.   4631-1

THE list of spiritual virtues is a familiar litany. Among them we find love, faith, hope, kindness, honesty, and sincerity. But there's one quality that Cayce often included to our dismay: long-suffering. We probably tend to draw back at that one, either because we simply don't want to suffer or because it stirs images of feeling sorry for ourselves.

What is it about the capacity to suffer that makes it so significant a virtue? Surely God wants us to be joyful, so why would any time spent in suffering be valuable?

Most of us spend a lot of time and energy avoiding questions like these. Often our hastiness is a rush to get away from uncomfortable—or even painful—situations. Take a look at your own life from this point of view. Do you fill up your daily schedule so completely that you don't have the time or energy to deal with something that would be painful to face? Do you ever feel as if you're hurrying through life—avoiding something that would probably be painful if you had to look directly at it?

Could it be that sometimes you don't slow down because you secretly believe that you'd suffer to do so?

These are hard questions. But notice Cayce's succinct advice to this woman's sincere appeal. His counsel is for her to be long-suffering. Something profound happens in us when we bear pain, sadness, and disappointment with courage. For one thing, it strengthens us in a way that nothing else can. Look back over your life, and undoubtedly you'll see in retrospect the positive effect that came out of some very troubling time. Giving birth is a painful process—not just the labor of birthing a baby, but the emergence *of anything new* in your life: physically, mentally, or spiritually.

But something equally important happens if we can bear our own burdens and suffer, without losing hope. *It connects us with other people who face similar pain.* We experience our *oneness.* Long-suffering—*if* it's understood as patient overcoming rather than indulgent self-pity—transforms us so radically that we really can be of help to others.

Who are the people to whom you can extend a helping hand? Aren't they the ones who now suffer in ways that you have suffered (or still do)? For example, the best addiction counselors are former addicts. The finest helpers to those returning from the trauma of war are those veterans who suffered through the same experience themselves.

It's an unusual triad that Cayce links for us: hastiness, long-suffering, and care for others. At first glance it may not be obvious how we get from compulsive busyness to compassion. However, by our courageous willingness simply to bear the pain that is already ours—and not necessarily go looking for more—we have the key to help each other.

Mini-motivator: Take time in your busy day to get in

touch with the areas in your life where there is pain. Then, without glorifying it or feeling sorry for yourself, have the courage to be conscious of your pain and bear it. Notice others around you who visibly or invisibly suffer. Recognize how your willingness to slow down and be long-suffering creates a bond with others.

Joy in Living

> ...fulfilling that purpose as He may have in thee is a greater service, a greater joy than may be had by him who may have builded a city or have conquered a nation ...
>
> 1129-2

$Y{ou}$ want your life to count for something. As a unique person, you want to matter.

But some days you probably feel very ordinary, as if you're just one of the masses. At those times it's difficult to determine whether or not your life is making much of a difference. Individuals no better nor more talented than you are making it into *People* magazine and popping up on the evening news. You may find yourself wondering, "Where did I go wrong? Why is my life so plain, so unremarkable?" You may feel as if you're meant for something special, but it all seems so vague, so elusive, and so out of reach.

This kind of worry uses the wrong standard of evaluation. Sure, you're meant for greatness—your own kind of greatness. But don't use public acclaim or notoriety to measure success. More often than not, the mass media *misses* what's really important in today's world—important from the angle of spirituality. What makes it into the mainstream news isn't necessarily what really makes a difference.

Truly *enjoying* your life—that is, finding joy in who you are and in what you do—requires only that you get in touch with your talents and then use them to help others whenever the opportunity arises. Don't concern yourself with doing some "great deed" that will make it into the history books. Don't let yourself be fooled into thinking that greatness means to "have builded a city or have conquered a nation," as Cayce put it.

So, what's *your* "gift"? Do you realize that you *are* gifted? That label isn't reserved for an elite few. Like each and every one, you've come into this life with certain talents, skills, and abilities. Those assets equip you to make a difference in the lives of many people. Is your gift to be a harmonizer—someone who gets people working together cooperatively? Is it to be the supporter—someone who sees the best in others and helps them reach their potential? Or is your "gift" to be an innovator—a person who is always ready to see things in a fresh, new way?

These are just examples of what Cayce called a personal mission. You're here on a mission, whether you've recognized it or not. Your soul's purpose involves contributing to the world around you and making a difference.

The *way* you do it may be small and unexceptional in the judgment of some people. But those individuals are simply using the wrong standard to measure you. You'll know you're really on track when life takes on a special flavor: rarely will you feel frantic; instead, you'll move purposefully through your day with assurance. Rarely will you get discouraged, even when things aren't going your way. You'll truly enjoy life and other people.

Joy. That's the mark of someone who has stopped looking for the world's approval and acclaim. Your life will radiate joy as you share yourself and your unique

Balancing Inner and Outer

For he that contributes only to his own welfare soon finds little to work for. He that contributes only to the welfare of others soon finds too much of others and has lost the appreciation of self, or of its ideals.   3478-2

RELATIONSHIPS can be a real headache sometimes. Rushing around, trying to keep everybody happy is a pain!

Do those words of frustration capture the way you feel some days? Don't worry, you're not alone. Virtually everybody has times when the strain of helping other people seems like too much. In fact, "burnout" is one of the hallmarks of contemporary living.

Headaches were literally a problem that plagued Lucille, and she found out from Cayce that it had a lot to do with her interpersonal relationships. At the age of sixty-six, she requested help with a long-standing problem of morning headaches. That appeal led to advice, not only about physical remedies, but also about getting along with people.

The recommendation—printed at the start of this chapter—came as a sort of modern proverb. In essence it says that living *just for yourself* gets you nowhere. You quickly discover that there's nothing meaningful for which to work. Life loses its vitality. Conversely, living *only for the sake of other people* doesn't work either. That kind of exclusive focus makes you stop appreciating your own genuine needs.

So, what's the answer? It's *balance.* It's maintaining an equilibrium that lovingly reaches out to others, but at the same time reserves sufficient time and energy for daily self-nurturance. In fact, that's the purpose of life, that's the essence of our spiritual challenge: to balance the outer and the inner—to harmonize (1) service to the needs of others with (2) attention to one's own require-ments. As Cayce told one thirty-six-year-old woman: " . . . ye are to fulfill the purpose for which each soul en-ters the earth—which is to manifest to the glory of God [that is, to love] and to the honor of self." (3333-1)

It's not selfish to take time for yourself. Doing so can save many a headache, literally and symbolically. To set aside the time and energy you need for staying healthy and centered (that is, "to honor yourself") prepares you for meeting others' needs.

How much is enough? How far can you go in meeting your own needs before you slip over into self-indul-gence? It's probably a little different each day. Balance certainly doesn't necessarily mean 50-50. Not many of us can afford to spend half the day attending to personal needs. On some days a reasonable investment might be half an hour for yourself for every dozen hours spent helping others. On other days, your own needs may be quite different and require more self-supportive time in order to keep a sense of balance.

Lucille got an important insight from Cayce about her headaches, and we can borrow her advice. Relationships should be a joy to us, not a source of aggravation. We can go a long way toward that goal if we remember the secret of a centered, happy life: balance.

Mini-motivator: Recognize one of your own needs today. Maybe it's for half an hour of time alone or for something special in your diet. Perhaps, it's a need to take a midafternoon nap or for time with a special person who inspires you. So that you can be your best self for others, invest the right amount of time and energy on whatever form of self-nurturance you choose.

One-Minute Meditation

(Q) How can I overcome the nerve strain I'm under at times?
(A) . . . Quiet, meditation, for a half [a minute] to a minute,
will bring strength . . .   311-4

WE live in a busy world, where time is at a premium for most people. Sometimes we may find ourselves asking, "How long will it take?" even before we ask, "And what will it cost?"

When time is tight, spiritual disciplines easily get overlooked or skipped. Perhaps there's no time in the morning to think about one's dreams, let alone write them down. When life is hectic, we probably don't follow the nutritional rules that we know are best for us. Meditation periods—which typically take twenty or thirty minutes of quality, stress-free attention—get squeezed out. How can one be a spiritual seeker and still live in a busy world?

Wouldn't it be wonderful if spiritual benefits could be derived from even brief investments of time and energy? Wouldn't it be nice if a good meditation could be done in only sixty seconds? In fact, it *is* possible to make an authentic contact with higher consciousness in a single minute.

This notion pushes some people's alarm button. There

are no shortcuts to enlightenment. Only by slow, steady effort does one progress to higher states of consciousness. In a world of fast foods and convenience stores, surely spiritual growth won't succumb to modern impatience as well!

But one-minute meditation doesn't necessarily imply shortcuts. No doubt the path to genuine enlightenment takes years of dedication, discipline, and commitment. But living in a time-demanding, hectic world doesn't mean you have to give up your meditation time. Some days it *is* possible to pause for twenty minutes. But on days when that goal is *not* achievable, you can see positive effects from even very short periods of silent, focused attention.

Here is one way to go about a mini-meditation session: Find a three-minute time slot when you're sure to be uninterrupted. You may even need to take the phone off the hook.

Spend the first minute on preparing for meditation. Do something that relaxes and centers you. One way might be through attentive breathing with your eyes closed, putting all your awareness on the rhythm of your breath. Experience yourself inhaling vitality and exhaling tension. You may even want to count silently and do about ten of these slow, deep breaths. That will take about a minute.

The next minute is spent in meditation: silent attention to your spiritual ideal. A helpful technique for many people is to focus on a short statement or affirmation of this highest value. Let your mind dwell completely on the feelings associated with that ideal. For example, your affirmation might be "I am a channel for peace in the world" or "The love of God fills me and flows out from me." Go with the spirit behind the words of your affirmation. Keep your attention on its deepest meaning.

Finally, spend a minute in healing prayer by sending out loving concern to others. Bless those individuals and surround them in light.

Mini-motivator: Pick a day that looks as if it's going to be really busy—a day when there are little or no prospects of setting aside twenty minutes or so for your regular meditation session. Instead—so as not to eliminate totally this important spiritual discipline from your day—try a mini-meditation. Be ready to experience the strength it can bring in the midst of the strain you're under.

Transcending Logic

Then see the joy, even in sorrow. See the pleasure that may even come with pain. These are mostly matters of the mind.   3440-2

WHAT kind of logic is this? Joy in sorrow, pleasure in pain? That sort of convoluted thinking doesn't sound very smart. Isn't logic one of the hallmarks of human development—the very talent that sets us apart from other creatures? It seems foolish to give it up.

What was Cayce getting at when he delivered this advice to Elizabeth, a twenty-nine-year-old woman who requested a reading to help her find happiness? Why did he invite her—even encourage her—to adopt such a radically different point of view? Apparently his spiritually clairvoyant angle on her life saw things in a way that doesn't seem too logical to us.

Maybe we're too wedded to rationality. On the one hand, it has given us extraordinary gifts, such as our advanced, comfortable life styles. But perhaps the intellect has tried to grab more authority than it deserves. The rational, logical aspect of the mind is jealous and doesn't want any competitors; it shuns other points of view about reality.

Logic can also contribute to our tension. Much of our

haste and worry are linked to rational demands. Little "voices" of logic are always whispering obligations. "You've got to get pregnant before you're forty or else the risks are too high." There's no arguing with that side of the mind. It's done its homework. The facts are there. *But that's not the only possible way to see your life!*

Notice what Cayce said to this young woman—to us all, for that matter. Things aren't always the way they seem. First impressions may not be the whole story, particularly ones that notice only appearances and judge by logic alone. Pain isn't always just discomfort. If we look deeper and see with the intuitive mind of the soul, we can sometimes discover pleasure: the delight that comes from courageously meeting a difficulty and growing through it.

Sorrow isn't always just sadness. A wiser view may see other things going on, too, which are "mostly matters of the mind," of one's consciousness. Seen with the intuitive, spiritually sensitive mind, there may also be joy: the elation of making an inner breakthrough in the face of anguishing problems.

No one is saying you ought to give up your intellect. The ability to think clearly and rationally is very valuable in today's world. Both material *and* spiritual growth can be enhanced by planning, analyzing, and thinking logically. But there's more to the story.

Stay flexible, stay open. Often things are more than they first appear to be. And you're equipped to see and understand that "something more." Trust your feelings and your intuitions, even when they are exactly opposite to logic. If they allow you to see a measure of joy in sorrow or a hint of pleasure in pain, don't worry—you haven't lost your mind. In fact, you've really *found* your mind: your soul-mind.

Mini-motivator: If you feel as if you've become too

wedded to your logical mind, ask for a temporary "separation agreement." You can still be friends with your intellect, but make it a point to listen to your intuitive mind as well. Pay attention to your feelings and hunches. Be alert for imaginative insights that may contradict logic.

Being Patient with Yourself

For few there be who comprehend that if they are patient first with their *own* selves they are then more capable of being . . . patient with others.   1158-2

EVERY day there is something a little bit different about you. This fact is easy to notice if you watch yourself carefully. You're continually changing, having a variety of cycles and rhythms. Your levels of creativity, vitality, enthusiasm, and health are constantly in flux. There are many factors: hormonal and other biological cycles, the weather, and maybe even esoteric elements such as astrological influences. When you lose touch with these variables, one result is almost sure to occur: impatience with yourself.

Take a close look at moments when you've been impatient. Probably what you'll see is that you got frustrated with your inability to do something as skillfully, as quickly, or as proficiently as you think you should. You haven't measured up to your own expectations. Maybe you're making careless errors in your work, or you're absent-mindedly forgetting a commitment. Perhaps that impatience with self is over a failure to change a character trait as fast as you think it ought to change.

No matter what form it takes, this sort of impatience

has a root cause: being out of touch with yourself as you really are that day. You've gotten out of sync with yourself. The demands you place on your own performance are inappropriate.

Overcoming self-impatience is *not* an invitation to laziness. It's *not* a matter of foregoing initiative and letting yourself drift, but it is a case of being tolerant. Some days you're better equipped for certain challenges; other days, a different type of task will be handled more smoothly.

Being patient with yourself fundamentally means greater sensitivity to the person you are today. It means listening inwardly and sensing your level of energy, alertness, and creativity—and then, setting goals for the day that fit those rhythms. For example, if you're writing a book, it's easy to get impatient when the words aren't flowing well. Maybe that's when another aspect of the overall task is more in sync with who you are that day— for example, editing previous drafts or doing background research.

Think about it: life might become rather dull if you were the same every day. Part of what makes your life interesting is variety. Once you accept the fact that you're a little bit different every day, then it becomes far easier to be patient with yourself. You can find a pace for the day and a set of challenges that you can really enjoy.

Mini-motivator: Before you decide on goals and plans for the day, take a self-inventory. Evaluate your mood, energy, health, and any other factors that seem important. Avoid any judgment; simply listen inwardly and feel who you are today. As much as possible, set a pace and rhythm for the day that will allow you to stay in sync with yourself and keep you from getting impatient.

Staying Open

Hence the more joy, the more *open activity* in the experience will bring greater and greater vision of beauty and harmony . . . [emphasis added]   1474-1

HOW open is your life? Do you already have an agenda for this day—one that leaves little room for anything unexpected? Even though you may think of yourself as a flexible, open-minded person, does that quality spill over into the way you run your life?

A little bit of careful, honest self-observation is likely to be surprising. You're apt to see that your day quickly gets filled up with obligations and demands. Just to cope with it all, you may find yourself defensively creating a plan for the day. That formula is a valiant attempt to keep everything organized, to make sure that you don't omit any "important" activity.

But as useful and necessary as a daily list of projects may be, something else often slips in: rigidity. The very aura around you becomes closed. Something in your being sends out a nonverbal message: "No more. I'm full up." That feeling is understandable, but then you miss much of what makes life meaningful. Without openness, life is just mechanical. It's lost its joy, its beauty, and its harmony.

With openness how might you meet the following kind of situation? (This is merely an example, but it serves as a type of parable of the modern, busy person.)

Imagine that you've got a jam-packed morning planned. There will be lots of stops to make and just enough time to do them all before you're due to a one o'clock doctor's appointment. Before all these stops, however, you'll be dropping off your next-door neighbor at her job. The two of you hardly ever have time to talk, so you didn't mind when she asked for a ride this particular day. You'll probably even enjoy the twenty-minute chat during the drive to her office.

But unexpectedly you get stuck in a traffic jam on the way. An accident has blocked both lanes of the road, and the two of you are likely to be stuck there for half an hour or more. How do you feel now? What are you going to do with this unforeseen event?

At first you probably feel frustrated. Now there's no way that everything on your list is going to get done. Feeling upset is normal. But how long does it last? How open can you be? *How willing are you to rediscover what this day is all about for you?* It takes a lot of flexibility to let go of a well-crafted plan. It's a special person who is so open that he or she is ready to be surprised by life and then gracefully adapt. Maybe that extra half an hour stuck in the car with your neighbor is a wonderful opportunity.

The Cayce readings offer a valuable promise to anyone willing to stay open: a vision of the beauty and harmony of life. You will begin to see situations and other people with different eyes. As helpful as agendas may occasionally be, sometimes it comes down to this basic question: What's more important today—completing everything on your list or enjoying the beauty and harmony of living? When it's put that way, the choice isn't too difficult.

Freedom from Worry

... worry will only unfit and prevent the body from meting out the best in self and for others, and in this respect *will* must *manifest* and not be pulled . . . about by circumstance, as it were.   39-4

TOM was worried. His feeling of security was rapidly slipping away. For months now, his financial picture had been getting more and more dismal. What made it even harder was that friends and colleagues weren't doing so badly. They seemed to be making it. "Something must be wrong with me," he thought.

Luckily, Tom had a resource to which he could turn. On three earlier occasions he had gotten help from Edgar Cayce, and this need seemed to justify another.

The reading from Cayce identified "conditions in the financial way and manner that present barriers, bugaboos, [and] fearful conditions . . . " (39-4) In other words, he was blocked. Fear and worry had created a resistant barrier that kept the best in him from getting out.

Where in your own life does worry stymie the best in you? If it's not finances—as it was with Tom—what issue *is* most likely to get you down? A troublesome relationship? Your health? Your career?

How can you deal with this dilemma, in whatever area of your life it exists? The answer is your free will—that ingredient of your soul which can break the vicious cycle of discouragement and despair created by worry. Your will is the faculty that can keep you from becoming a slave to unpredictability and misfortune.

Take a close look at what's going on when you slip into *chronic* worry. Some small degree of anxious concern is probably unavoidable, living in the kind of world we do. But notice what happens when continual fretting takes hold of you. You become "pulled . . . about by circumstances," as Cayce put it, and your sense of well-being and self-esteem is shaped—not by an inner strength—but by outer events. You're like a marionette puppet at the mercy of situations and happenings.

Here's where your free will can come to the rescue, *if* you keep in mind this extraordinary resource. When Cayce gave his advice to Tom—and to all of us who struggle with the effects of worry—he wasn't referring to so-called "willpower," which merely tries to use coercion to force its own way. The will of the soul is, instead, *an inner strength that allows each one of us to remember something special about ourselves.* Perhaps more important than anything else about the will is its ability to put us back in touch with "the best in self."

The next time you catch yourself in a downward cycle of worry and fear, try this. First, recognize that you've been letting events and conditions control you, unconsciously shaping your attitudes and feelings. Once you can see clearly what's been happening rather automatically, then take the next step to get yourself out of that destructive rut. You've got the inner power to decide who you are and what your life is about. Use that ability *to remember your best self.* Use your free will to call forth some memories of previous successes.

The difficulties and challenges at hand may not disappear immediately. But when you approach them with a strong sense of your best self, a solution won't be far off.

Mini-motivator: Break a worry cycle by using your free will. For one day try meeting a specific problem from the area of strength. Whenever you catch yourself starting to worry, use your will to stop that training of thought and insert a replacement: choose to remember the best self that lives in you. Then, turn your attention back to the difficulty, but now with a more positive outlook.

Continuity of Life

Be patient even in those periods of exaltation, joy, sorrow, woe. For in [patience] do all become aware of the *continuity* of life itself . . .
705-2

TAKE a moment and say these words silently to yourself: "I am forever. I am . . . forever." Get a sense of something eternal within you—your spiritual identity that can say to itself "I am." Simply feel the reality of yourself as an immortal soul. Try it now. "I am . . . forever."

Surely that feeling is quite different from the ones that usually grab for your attention—impatience, worry, discouragement. It's a sad fact that modern living doesn't put us in touch with spiritual truth, as the contemporary world has different values and priorities.

Too often there's a mad scramble to attain poor substitutes for our real needs. Modern living tries to make us believe that being physically secure and comfortable ought to satisfy us, that it ought to be a reasonable substitute for our authentic spiritual longings. Unfortunately, the rewards of materialism offer at best only a stop-gap satisfaction, a temporary band-aid to the wounds of the soul.

But if you can separate yourself from hurried schedules and discouraging newspaper reports, you can make this remarkable rediscovery: life is continuous. Something deep within your being knows about the continuity of life.

With that remembrance, suddenly something changes about the way you live your day. You have time for people. The individuals you encounter aren't an aggravation or a distraction. You have time to listen to someone's story. You have time to go out of your way to help. Those unexpected intrusions that used to make you tense now take on a different flavor.

Remembering the continuity of life—one's own immortality—brings into sharp focus just how misguided so many of our plans and projects really are. Many of our compulsions and drives are masks for our doubts and fears. The periods when tasks just *have* to get done by a certain time are actually our distorted attempts to prove something. We mistakenly think we have to justify our own worthiness and erroneously act as if we had to earn God's love by impressive deeds.

Continuity of life is *already* ours. We can relax. Sure there's work to be done, lots of work. But those tasks aren't intended to prove ourselves or to earn something. What we're all truly looking for, whether we recognize it or not, is the assurance that life will always continue. When we accept that it does—when we trust that inner feeling that life really is continuous—then our way of being with others is radically altered. Compassion becomes natural. A relaxed, forgiving manner comes easy. A steady assurance carries us patiently through the challenges of the day.

Mini-motivator: Try living this day with the following affirmation in the back of your mind: "Life is continuous—I am forever." With that assurance, be willing to let go of any hurried compulsions and to have time for people.

Fullness of Time

And let not thy heart be troubled; ye believe in God. Believe in His promises, too, that as ye sow, so in the fullness of time and in material experience these things shall come about.   1968-5

INSTANTITIS. You'll never find that word in the dictionary, but it's an apt description of the plague of modern life. We're infected with the mistaken notion that things ought to happen instantly. We have a spiritual dis-ease of impatience.

The influences that keep this collective illness going are potent—and often subtle. We're easily hypnotized by impressions that events can happen quickly. Television dramas resolve problems in a single hour—feature-length movies, in about two. Jetliners whisk us from coast to coast in four hours, a journey that our ancestors would have been lucky to make in four months.

These hypnotic effects trick us into expecting something that's actually unrealistic. We come to believe that change—any sort of change—should occur *when* we want it and however *quickly* we want. It's no wonder that we get fooled and then end up frustrated. After all, computer data can be altered instantly with a keystroke. Blood pressure can be manipulated by swallowing a pill.

Why shouldn't troublesome character traits be changed just as quickly? Or interpersonal relationships? Or unwanted attitudes? Or unhealthy habits?

But human souls aren't like computer data banks. Real-life friendships and communities aren't made of the same stuff as television programs. The spiritual fabric of our lives doesn't operate with a hurried sense of clock time. It changes and unfolds with its own rhythm. And if we want to be healed of "instantitis," we've got to learn to be sensitive to this deeper pattern of how things are transformed.

From a spiritual point of view, events change when the time is right—or, as the Bible often puts it, "in the fullness of time." At first, this may sound like the unsatisfying answer we used to get from our parents. In response to our impatient questions, we might have been told that changes would come when the time was right. As children, that probably meant that our parents simply didn't know when or that it was all too complicated to explain.

But "the fullness of time" isn't necessarily a phrase to mask ignorance or keep secrets. Instead, it can point to the fact that much of what makes change possible goes on behind the scenes. A lot of the work happens at invisible levels, just as the development of an embryo is concealed within the mother's body. Birth is the dramatic moment that reveals the countless little changes that went on for months out of sight. As we know, the birth of a healthy child can come only when the time is right.

It works the same way in your own life with the changes you'd like to see happen. A new career track, better communications in the family, more stable finances. Whatever alteration you're looking for, remember that it can come only "in the fullness of time." Lots of little changes are, in fact, going on invisibly as you clarify your purposes, work with your attitudes, and act on the best you know to be doing. Behind the scenes the time is drawing nearer for the birth of something new in your life.

Mini-motivator: Recognize how "instantitis" shapes your expectations. Then select a specific change you're hoping for in your life. Try to nurture a new way of feeling about that part of your life—a willingness to do your part, but also to trust that the changes will come when the time is right.

Being Fully Present

The greater an individual, the more content an individual may be.   347-2

"NEXT!"

Is there any other word that, with punctuated emphasis, better characterizes modern life? We're continually hurried along by it.

"Next in line. Come on, move along!"

"Stay tuned for scenes from next week's exciting episode."

"This is so boring . . . what comes next?"

Strong forces—both inside ourselves and from the surrounding world—are always trying to keep us focused on what's to follow. An inner restlessness makes us want to escape from the here and now as soon as possible. Why can't we be fully present to *this* moment? Why must our attention be continually drawn to the future?

No doubt there are many reasons for our attempts to escape from the present moment. But whatever those excuses may be, one fact is inescapable: True enjoyment of living can happen only in the now. We're never happy when we're trying to avoid ourselves and bypass our lives the way they are right now.

Edgar Cayce's philosophy refers frequently to contentment: the continuing ability to find peace and meaning in the current situation. He called it a measure of one's greatness—an indicator of one's inner development and understanding.

Contentment isn't satisfaction; it isn't a willingness to settle for the status quo. It leaves room for the desire for growth and improvement. But contentment recognizes and appreciates that what's happening right now is meaningful—worth being experienced fully and without any compulsion to move on to what's next.

To be content you must learn to say to yourself, "I'm in no hurry for this experience to end." Of course, that's easy when the event or situation is pleasant. It's a much bigger challenge when things are uncomfortable or even painful. This slogan of contentment—"I'm in no hurry for this experience to end"—does *not* equate to resignation; it's not a matter of giving in to unhappy circumstances. Instead, it's an affirmation of two spiritual principles:

- What's going on right now is purposeful, and
- Nothing's going to change permanently unless we listen to and appreciate the lessons that life brings us.

The irony of contentment is that paradoxically things *do* start to change for the better. It's all because of a willingness to stay with the moment and experience the fullness of what it offers. When we fight something and wish it would pass quickly, it has the opposite effect: The burden seems interminable.

Give contentment a chance in your life. Try it out. Even though it sometimes seems to invite prolonged discomfort, the way you will begin to experience events may surprise you. Try saying to yourself when caught in a traffic jam, "I'm in no hurry for the light to turn green," and really mean it. Or when your mind starts wandering to your next appointment, try saying to yourself, "I'm in no rush for this meeting to end."

The secret is to use this affirmation as a trigger. It serves to put you in touch with the positive possibilities and the deeper meaning of the present moment—something your busy, impatient mind may prefer to avoid.

Mini-motivator: Dedicate one day especially to contentment. Don't be so concerned about what comes next. Be willing to accept and appreciate the present moment and all it brings.

PART TWO

ATTAIN PEACE AND SURRENDER FEAR

. . . until ye are willing to lose thyself in service, ye may not indeed know that peace which He has promised to give — to all.   1599-1

Introduction

Peace is probably the most elusive quality of life. For a fleeting moment on a hectic day, you may find the time to relax. Then it's back to all your demanding responsibilities. Or for a few days you might get away from the noisy bustle of modern living and discover a little peace and quiet. But all too soon, the tranquillity evaporates as you have to return to the real world.

Our needs for peace reach inward, too. Worries, doubts, and fears destroy peace of mind and heart. Just when we think we've found inner stability, something comes along to throw us off balance.

Of the thousands of people who came to Edgar Cayce for advice, most were looking for peace. They may not have always posed their questions in those terms. But their troubled souls and wounded bodies were calling out for something that would bring them peace.

Cayce's approach to peace was clearly a spiritual one. The philosophy of life found in the readings points to an invisible realm of the spirit as the place where all peace begins. From that basic assumption, two ideas are right at the heart of his message about peace.

First, *everything is trying to move toward peace.* As he put it in his reading for one woman, "The whole of God's creation seeks harmony and peace!" (1742-4) Of course, that isn't always obvious when we look at life from our own, limited perspective. A lot of what goes on seems anything but an impulse toward greater peace. But maybe we need to learn how to see more deeply the motives and purposes that guide human affairs. Perhaps, as an undercurrent to everything, we'd discover the desire for peace.

Second, Cayce offers us a hopeful idea: *God has prom-*

ised peace to each of us. In fact, promises were something that came up time and again when Cayce counseled people about their troubled, painful, fearful lives. "Peace . . . is the greater promise that has ever been made to man," Cayce told one individual (543-11). Peace is promised to us. Of course, it takes some effort on our part to claim that assurance. We've got to hold up our end of the bargain. We've got to be willing to put aside our worries and our fears, allowing room for the peace that was pledged to us.

Claiming the promise is what this section is all about. Each chapter addresses ways to get rid of fear and help you find peace of mind and heart.

Birthright

Only in casting thyself wholly upon the Lord may ye know
the spiritual and mental peace that is the birthright of every
soul. Only in defying same . . . ye become entangled in
confusion, doubt and fear.   1326-1

WHAT belongs to you from birth? What advantages are
inherently yours—not political privileges, but spiritual
rights? What experiences are yours for the asking, simply because you're a creation of God?

Peace is one of them. It's the birthright of every soul to
have peace. Why, then, do so many throw away this privilege? In thousands of little ways people all over the world
have chosen to defy this right. They have unwittingly
given up the spiritual advantage that would transform
the troubles of physical life.

Maybe the gift of peace is too hard for us to accept. If
we think it's something we're supposed to earn—like
other rewards that come from our accomplishments—
then we probably don't feel worthy. Knowing that we
haven't always acted very peacefully ourselves, we don't
feel as if we deserve much peace in return.

But spiritual law doesn't always follow conventional
wisdom. Sometimes the rules that God has set up for us
don't follow the logic we'd expect. Whether we deserve it

or not, some things are ours simply by wanting them. That's what a birthright means. And inner peace is at the top of the list.

Sylvia had lost touch with this principle. When she contacted Edgar Cayce for advice, she was in a state of despair. After three-and-a-half years of a troubled marriage, she and Jacob had separated. Now just a few weeks after he had left, she discovered she was pregnant with his child. She wanted Cayce's spiritual counsel: Should she attempt to win her husband back, and if so, how?

You don't have to win back anything, was the advice. The marriage may, in fact, be worth redeeming. But be careful in your approach. The harmony that you want isn't locked up inside your estranged husband. Peace is already yours. It's your birthright. Don't get caught in a game that you think you can win or lose.

How often do you remember that principle when you're troubled? How often do you think someone else holds the key to your own state of peace or turmoil? Instead, you can claim what's rightfully yours. Peace is already yours, just for the asking. It's not a question of deserving it, earning it, or winning it back. It's your birthright.

Mini-motivator: Simply claim peace for yourself today: peaceful thoughts, peaceful feelings, and a peaceful way of going about your duties. It belongs to you. No one can take it away from you. Keep that spiritual law in mind.

Inspiration

. . . no emergency in a material way or manner may arise that may not find its counterpart in a spiritual inspiration.

877-7

ROGER was at the top of his profession. As a corporate lawyer in New York City, he had made it big. At the age of forty-four he was co-owner of a seat on the New York Stock Exchange and was the envy of many. He had a solid marriage, reliable friends—and since having met Edgar Cayce several years earlier, he also had a meaningful spiritual direction for his life.

But in the spring of 1936, Roger was caught in fear. He had made a momentous decision to sell both his expensive waterfront home and his share of the brokerage firm. He was ready for something different; he felt that his soul *had to have* a change. He wasn't exactly sure what was next for him, but he had some ideas. Maybe teaching and writing. Perhaps trying to help other people more directly by working as a counselor.

But before anything like that could be explored, he had to find buyers for his large assets. He needed that money to sustain his family while he found his new way in the months ahead. Of course, it might not be easy in the economic hard times of the mid-1930s. So he began to grow afraid. Rather than be hopeful and excited about his recent prospects, he was beginning to let fear control his thinking. What if he couldn't find purchasers? What if he was simply deluding himself about being ready for another career?

The fear and doubt were becoming so strong that he turned to Cayce for advice. Words of encouragement came in that reading: an invitation to surrender his fears and be open to a calming inspiration. Hold fast to the sense of life purpose that you've been feeling from your inner self, Cayce told him. Expect that people will offend you and that situations won't always seem to be going your way during this transition. But when doubt creeps in, remember that for every crisis or physical emergency, there is a counterbalancing inspiration. It will lift your spirits and quiet your troubled mind. To help you keep in touch with that possibility—to help you surrender your fears—use this visualization method: Imagine Jesus on the turbulent sea with His disciples and how He calmed the troubled waters.

When the typed transcript of the reading arrived at his home, it must have made a lot of sense to Roger. In a personal note back to Cayce that week he wrote: "The reading was perfect; I understand exactly what was meant, all the way through."

Something about this principle of inspiration rang true for him. Perhaps it does for us, too. No matter what kind of fearful emergency or anxious test we're facing, there's an antidote. Just as surely as modern physics teaches "for every action there's an equal and opposite reaction," so too does our inner life behave lawfully. In the depths of our anxiety and worry, something else is offered to us from the heights. When we're most seriously caught up in fear, that's when we have the best chance to feel the calming, strengthening power of God.

Mini-motivator: The next time a crisis or problem makes you fearful, pause and let the image of Christ calming the waters lift your spirits. Claim the promise that whenever you're at a low point, an inspiration is there waiting for you.

Avoiding Antagonism

(Q) Will the attacks come to naught that have been made on me by the American Medical Association?
(A) Depends upon the antagonistic attitude that the body assumes . . . If ye would have peace, be peaceful!   969-1

PETER was a man ahead of his times. Born in the last year of the Civil War, he had grown up to see his world change immeasurably. He had followed a career in medicine at a time when the modern field was just beginning to establish itself. In the early years of his profession, there was still considerable flexibility. New discoveries were occurring all the time. New therapies were competing for favor, and Peter open-mindedly embraced anything that offered help to his patients.

As his experience and skills expanded, he became a spokesman for several of the new methods, including chiropractic manipulation and iridology (diagnostic techniques using the iris of the eye). He wrote articles and lectured extensively about his medical beliefs. Some people admired his breadth of vision and openness. Others thought he was naive and gullible, risking his license as an M.D.

Conditions began to change for Peter as he neared the end of his career. By the 1930s what we now know as mainstream allopathic medicine had gained favor in America. There was little or no tolerance for alternative therapies. The American Medical Association was a powerful force trying to limit mavericks like Peter. He dreamed of opening a training institute in Washington, D.C.—a school of universal medicine. The AMA bureaucrats dreamed of forcing Peter into retirement.

By the time he turned to Cayce for some advice, he was in hot water. An investigation was under way. The AMA felt that it was simply trying to protect the public from an irresponsible doctor. He felt as if he were under attack from a close-minded organization that didn't really have his patients' best interests in mind. What was his proper line of defense? What kind of truce was possible so that peace could be reestablished in his professional life?

Cayce's clairvoyant view of the problem described a remedy. It began with Peter's own attitude. Even though his words and behaviors were mild-mannered, inwardly he was agitated—even antagonistic. His mind was often filled with imagined arguments with AMA officials. He was mentally plotting his next moves in the conflict.

Stop your belligerent attitude, Cayce advised. If you're mentally creating a showdown, you'll get one. By the law of attraction, antagonism in the outer world will come forth to meet your inner antagonism. But you can cut off the process. From your own mind you can stop feeding the growing battle. If you want peace, be peaceful—especially in your thoughts.

Haven't we all faced struggles like Peter's? Maybe they haven't been so severe that our means of livelihood was in jeopardy. But upon careful reflection, we're likely to see that a similar process was at work. Our own antagonistic thoughts and feelings kept reinforcing the fight. Thus, our inner hostility was met by an outer one. We can only speculate whether the situation might have turned out differently if we had broken the self-perpetuating sequence.

Mini-motivator: The next time you sense an impending conflict, do your part to stop the process cold. Refuse to be pulled into the friction. Cut off your thoughts of attack. Give peace a chance by being peaceful inwardly.

Casting Out Fear

Reduce this fear in the body by the meditation and prayer. Begin especially with those portions of the scripture that refer to promises to the individual that there is within self that which casts out fear . . .   4072-1

ROBERT felt hopelessly out of place in his world. All of his friends were overseas serving in the military in World War II. And he was at home with a strange ailment that disqualified him, an illness that also kept him from being very productive with his tremendous talents as an artist. Life seemed bleak to this twenty-six-year-old man.

His unusual physical problem began when he was twelve: an episode of severe muscle spasms. The family doctor thought it was simply the result of something he had eaten, but five years later the condition began recurring frequently, this time in a more serious form. Now the spasms led to fainting spells and brief comas.

The family consulted many specialists but with no success. He was hospitalized and X-rayed from head to toe. He was tested for allergies. But every report came back with the same conclusion: he seemed to be perfectly fit. Even the physicians at the Mayo Clinic concluded that there was nothing they could do for him because they couldn't determine the cause of these spells. Robert and his family were up against a blank wall.

As a last resort they agreed to try the suggestion of Robert's cousin. She had read about Edgar Cayce in an article published by *Coronet* magazine. In their letter requesting a reading, only a single question was posed: What causes his fainting spells or comas?

As he had on thousands of other occasions, Cayce offered a clairvoyant diagnosis from hundreds of miles away. He saw that at a physical level the condition came from poor eliminations. Congestions in the bowel were triggering reactions in the nervous and endocrine systems. Treatments were recommended: castor oil packs, massage, and dietary changes.

But then Cayce addressed the deeper issue: What was the cause of those imbalances in his eliminations? Fear played a major role. If Robert wanted to experience a total healing, it would mean overcoming his fears. For him, one of the best ways to do this would be through meditating on specific portions of the Bible. The fourteenth through seventeenth chapters of the Gospel of John were particularly recommended. Here Robert would find promises. In these passages we all can find spiritual reassurance to begin to conquer our fears.

Mini-motivator: Take about ten minutes for each of four consecutive days to try Cayce's remedy for fear. Each of those days read one of the four chapters from John. At the end of your reading time, take a few more minutes to think about the verses in that chapter that were most meaningful to you.

Meditative Peace

Learn that quiet first within self, from within . . . wherein
there may be the peace . . .   694-2

MEDITATION is like an oasis of peace in the midst of
hectic schedules and worrisome responsibilities. In
those ten or twenty minutes of daily quiet, it's possible
to keep yourself centered and tranquil.

But anyone who has tried to keep a regular meditation discipline knows that it doesn't always work quite as
well as expected. There are days when you may get up
from your meditation session and feel no more peaceful
than you did when you sat down. What's gone wrong on
days like that?

The trouble is most likely the *approach*—the very attitude with which you tried to meditate. If you've carried
with you into meditation the familiar mind-set of daily
life, then the results from your meditation will probably
be frustrating. If you've tried to transplant into your session your competitive, acquisitive approach to life, you
will have discovered that it doesn't work for meditation.

What is this familiar approach to life that is so ill-
suited for meditation? Throughout most of our waking
hours we're striving—even straining—to reach goals and
accomplish tasks. We're attempting to acquire things,

like physical possessions or people's approval. Often, our efforts are tinged with competition as we try to prove ourselves. Simply put, we're trying to get something.

But what happens if you attempt to carry that approach with you into meditation the same way you try to earn the boss's approval at work or to complete a trip to the grocery store in less than an hour? It backfires. That straining, acquisitive attitude is the very opposite of authentic meditation.

Without realizing it, your meditation life can turn into an extension of your daily life. It's a subtle thing, but that's probably the reason many people go through dry spells in which meditation just doesn't seem to work for them anymore.

Watch what can happen if "acquiring peace" has become the goal of meditation just like all the other goals of material life. You sit down for your quiet time, and already you have in mind what you want: peace of mind. It's a commodity, just like a loaf of bread from the store or a larger return on your stock investment. It's something you want and now you're going to use a technique to get it. Concentrating very hard on your mantra or affirmation, you go on the hunt. You're stalking peace. It's hiding somewhere in the fortress of your unconscious. But you think that the power of your focused mind will track it down. Surely within ten minutes peace will belong to you. Sad to say, after ten, twenty, or even thirty minutes, you're no closer to peace. You get up from your meditation vaguely frustrated and unsatisfied.

So, what *will* work? What's the right approach if you want to experience peace through meditation? The key is *giving* rather than getting. It's a matter of surrendering yourself. Surrendering your worries. Being willing to give up your expectations, and not expecting to get anything—*not even peace*. The whole purpose of this meditation session is *to give.*

Sitting down for your quiet period, you may choose to use a mantra or affirmation. But those words simply help you open your feelings to something bigger than yourself. You're not out to get something; you're offering yourself to God. "Here I am. I give up . . . my fears . . . my worries. I surrender . . . my agenda . . . my sense of what's needed."

That basic attitude of turning yourself over to God is the heart of genuine meditation. It's not a technique; it's not a clever maneuver in consciousness. It is simply the offering of oneself. From that surrendering comes a byproduct: the peace of God. What a strange paradox. It's only when you're willing to give up the goal of *acquiring* peace that the *gift* of peace is presented to you.

Mini-motivator: For today's meditation period, take a new approach. Put aside all your expectations about what you might get out of the meditation session. Don't worry about your "performance" as a meditator. For today the whole purpose of those ten or twenty minutes will be surrender. You'll openly offer yourself to God.

Peace Through Self-Knowledge

... those that seek to know self may find the way. Those that find the way become content, and find joy, peace . . . 352-1

SOMETHING starts to change in late adolescence. A light at the end of the tunnel comes into view. Those middle teenage years have been a confusing mix of emotions and demands. Then, at age seventeen or eighteen, the seed of one's adult self begins to emerge. The quest for self-knowledge begins to bear fruit. Of course, it's a search that will extend into one's twenties and thirties—in fact, it will reach throughout a lifetime. With each step in self-knowledge can come a little more peace of mind and heart.

Teenage life for a girl like Katherine in the 1930s was a lot different than for adolescents in our own times. Those years included the depths of the Depression. Gender roles were still rigid, and career opportunities for young women were severely limited. Just the same, life in that time wasn't as complex as it is now, and there weren't as many distractions and temptations.

But if we put aside all the differences, what remains is a theme of late adolescent life that's as old as humanity itself: the restless search to know oneself and to shape an independent identity for the adult years ahead. Peace of mind doesn't come easily when you're young and trying to find out who you are.

Katherine was fortunate that her family knew about Edgar Cayce and obtained a reading to help her through that transition period. The information she received at age seventeen was a boost to her self-esteem and a challenge for her future. It emphasized her talents, such as her scholastic abilities in French. She had proven herself time and again with her accomplishments at school. Now she'd face a test in the years immediately ahead.

Her life's path would soon come to a fork, Cayce predicted. One way would involve using her considerable skills in self-indulgent, self-serving ways. The alternative meant putting those talents to constructive use by aiding others, even though it would sometimes require sacrifice. Only one way would lead to peace and contentment.

This fork in the road wasn't to be a single moment in Katherine's future. It would be a type of choice she'd face repeatedly. In many of those situations it wouldn't be immediately obvious which way would lead to peace. There wouldn't always be signposts to mark neatly the options. Only from careful self-study would she be able to recognize the way; only through self-knowledge would she be able to see the path to a peaceful life.

Cayce's advice to Katherine was meant to last a lifetime. *But it's just as applicable to any of us today—*whether we're seventeen, forty-seven, or seventy-seven. If we want to create a peaceful life, there's always one requirement: Know thyself. Without an understanding of ourselves, we'll constantly fall prey to self-deception and the turmoil it always produces. Without a basis of self-understanding, our decisions will be hit-or-miss, creating instability and uncertainty. Peace begins with self-knowledge.

Mini-motivator: Invest fifteen to thirty minutes today doing something that helps you get to know yourself better. For example, your exercise in self-understanding might be to work on interpreting one of your recent dreams. Or it might be trying something new—some activity that has never fit your familiar self-image—and seeing how it makes you feel.

Not as the World Gives Peace

" . . . My peace I give unto thee—not as the world giveth peace" in the gratifying . . . or of looking for ease and comfort irrespective of that it may bring into the experiences of others . . .   1440-1

HOW does the world give peace? What did Jesus mean when He contrasted His kind of peace with the sort that comes from material life? The biblical account isn't very explicit. We're left to figure it out for ourselves—or to turn to insightful interpreters such as Cayce.

First, we might well wonder what qualifies this man to comment on an enigmatic teaching of Jesus. Certainly Cayce had no formal theological training. But the Bible was the centerpiece of his life. He read it cover to cover more than sixty times. He prayed with it, he dreamed about its characters, he taught its principles in Sunday school for all his adult years. Because it was so much a part of his conscious and unconscious life, some of his greatest work as a psychic was making the Bible come alive for people.

Here we have the most important passage in the New Testament about peace. "My peace I give unto thee—not as the world giveth peace." (John 14:27) Surely, if we're ever to understand peace from a spiritual angle, we've got to decipher this statement. Why is the mundane sort of peace so much less than the peace of God?

Cayce elaborates for us. Seeming to move for a moment into Jesus' frame of mind, Cayce adds a description of the inferior form of peace—peace as the world gives. It's a kind of self-complacence that puts personal ease and comfort first. In other words, there is a type of peace that allows one person to have it easy while someone else pays the price. That lucky one who gets the benefit is more likely than not quite willing to stay ignorant of what's really happening.

This very idea is sure to make many of us anxious. If we're members of the privileged class in society, we've probably come to expect the right to certain comforts. We may say to ourselves, "I work hard and I deserve what I've got." But *sometimes* the ease that makes our lives feel a little more peaceful comes at the expense of someone else.

This is hard to accept and face. For example, those of us in the Western world, especially in America, consume a vastly disproportionate share of the earth's resources. Even *within our own country* millions of people go to bed each night hungry and/or inadequately sheltered. If it's too overwhelming to think about such problems on this big a scale, perhaps you can still find examples in the smaller circle of your own family and community. Are there times when you get comfortable benefits at the expense of someone else?

This is part of Cayce's message about peace that can distress us. Sometimes we'd probably prefer his philosophy to stay focused on metaphysics and abstract universal law. We begin to squirm a little when the readings start talking about being our brother's and sister's keeper. The social and moral dimensions of Cayce's philosophy have all too often been ignored.

But this is an unavoidable part of genuine peace. Cayce asks us to believe that Jesus was calling us to a radical reevaluation of how we go about our lives. It suggests that there's a superficial kind of peace that comes from comfort and ease. It's actually a bogus form of peace—a caricature of what peace can really be. What makes it an illusory peace? It's not so much that the comforts of the world are wrong—the problem is when they come at the expense of others. In those cases, something deep in our souls knows it's not fair. Consciously we may be relaxed and pleased with ourselves, but at our core there's a restless knowing that something's not right.

So what do we do? Feeling guilty about eating a good dinner tonight isn't the answer. Nor is any other form of guilt. What's called for is a willingness to be aware. That sounds simple, but it's not easy. It's a brave person who is able to see how *some* of his or her comforts might be linked to a burden for someone else. It takes courage to recognize how we occasionally settle for the lesser form of peace even though it brings no peace to our souls.

Mini-motivator: Take a careful look at what makes your life easy and comfortable. Try to see how you get a superficial peace of mind or body at the expense of someone else. Simply coming to that awareness is the biggest step. Next, do something—even just a little something at first—that would ease that burden.

The Will to Peace

...peace...comes from making *thy* will one with Creative Forces—which is love! 1792-2

THE world was moving toward war. It was 1939 and events in Europe were growing more ominous every month. The terrible war that was coming would surely be a test of wills, but it would also be a test of machines and technology.

Joseph was one of a handful of scientists and engineers whose secret work would eventually turn the course of that war. He would become a key member of the Manhattan Project team that would create the first atomic bomb.

But in 1939 it was hard for him to see the significant role in human history he would play. Joseph was discouraged and his self-esteem was sagging. When he wrote to Cayce and asked for a reading, he was hoping for something that would lift his spirits and get his life refocused in a meaningful way.

It is, perhaps, ironic that one of the most succinct statements about peace in all the Cayce readings was given to this man, one of the builders of the atomic bomb. In fact, the statement was preceded by a warning because Cayce described previous lives in which his scientific and engineering skills had been put to the test. More than once before his soul had faced the question of using scientific abilities for either good or evil.

However, the reading didn't threaten Joseph or give him any ultimatums or try to intimidate him to quit his job. Instead, it talked of peace and of finding peace in his own life.

Peace is essentially an act of your will, the reading told him. It comes from a willingness to let love guide your life. Peace requires an act of will that surrenders—not out of discouragement and defeat—but out of knowledge that there's a better way than your own automatic tendencies. Peace means allowing something bigger than yourself to work through you. It means letting go of your own agenda.

Think about what this message for Joseph also means to *you*. If peace is linked to your will, then it gradually emerges from the little choices that you make every day. It's a matter of the small decisions—the ones that could happen almost impulsively, if you're not careful. When you feel a dispute bubbling up with a colleague, do you push willfully for your own way? Or do you let go and invite love to be a guide? If you're not careful and attentive enough, things could move fast and before you know it the contentious bickering has begun.

If you've just been disappointed by a friend and you feel ready to lash out in resentment, what do you do with your will? There's always the possibility of putting your hurt feelings in perspective and letting love direct you. That's when peace happens.

Mini-motivator: Spend a day carefully paying attention to the little choices that you make. Notice when you have an option between pushing for your own way or letting go and allowing love to guide the situation. Choose love that day. Decide to willingly allow some-

thing bigger than your normal reactions to be in charge.
Be an agent of peace.

Spreading Peace

Such peace as the world, or the rabble, knoweth not . . .
every thought, every act, becomes a *song* in the heart . . .
272-7

BY now it seemed too late to turn back. Theresa's marriage had been going downhill for years and now it was at a breaking point. Her husband Bennett was seemingly too busy with his fast-paced, lucrative career as an attorney. He complained that he just didn't have the time and energy for the sort of marriage she wanted.

It wasn't going to be the end of the world for her. She had her own career as a sixth-grade teacher. It would mean a step-down in her style of living since she couldn't afford to maintain their expensive home on her salary alone. But she knew that she'd make do in a more modest setting.

Most of all she wanted to make sure that this next phase of her life—the post-divorce period—went in the right direction. So she wrote to her friend Edgar Cayce. She'd known about him for many years, having first heard about his readings in a college classroom. She had received readings on six previous occasions in years past. In fact, Theresa had become a supporter of his work, sending contributions when she heard that finances were tight.

What would this longtime friend and source of sound

advice tell her? First, her reading assured her that parting ways with her husband was best. She had tried everything she could do, and now it was time to move on with her life.

Then, as she had found in her previous readings from Cayce, there was an inspiring message of hope. In explicit terms the reading described her spiritual calling in life. She could be a builder of peace in her world. She had a knack for spreading peace. To do so she would have to resist the temptation to go to either of two extremes. One was trying to make a big name in the world—to be someone of notoriety who would influence people in a dramatic way. The other extreme was to withdraw from the world and try to bring peace by quiet solitude. She was warned against these two detours with the words: "Not any great revelation, not in the fanfare of trumpet, not in segregating self from the world . . . " (272-2)

Her life's mission as an agent of peace was to take a middle road. Her gift was in meeting the everyday challenges with a song in her heart. Her special talent was helping people see how troubles and difficulties could be met with *a lightness of spirit.* Because she was innately so good at doing that, her influence would easily transfer from one person to the next. One individual whose troubled mind was made more peaceful by Theresa would naturally do the same for someone else. Like a chain reaction, dozens of people every day would experience more peace.

Even though this was Theresa's special gift, to some degree we're all capable of triggering chain reactions of peace. Every day we impact other people—for better *or* for worse—and the influence we impart gets passed on. If we set our minds to it, we can confront difficult situations with songs in our hearts and spread peace wherever we go.

Mini-motivator: The next time a problem comes up in relationship to other people, meet that event with a lightness of spirit. Be a trigger for peace. Feel how your positive attitude is going to have an effect indirectly on many other people today as a peaceful chain reaction is set in motion.

Meeting Christ

... "Though ye wander far afield, call upon the Lord while He may be found and He will draw very nigh unto thee; and with His presence bring peace."   294-174

THE atmosphere was sometimes tense in the Cayce household. The demands on everyone's time and energy were extraordinary. Money was usually in short supply, and small tensions and jealousies surfaced from time to time among the supporters who tried to help Edgar Cayce. On occasion those difficulties would culminate in a major setback, such as the bickering that led to the collapse of the Cayce Hospital in 1928 and the failure of Atlantic University in 1930.

But on other occasions the tension was more subtle, like an undercurrent of frustration. In April of 1934, Cayce himself arranged for a reading about the situation. He knew it was time to get back on track. Little squabbles and misunderstandings were diverting attention from the real work at hand.

The message offered from his superconscious mind spoke of peace—the most profound kind of peace that humanity could experience. The Christ was at hand. If Cayce and his immediate followers would be alert to experience that Presence, the entire situation would be dramatically transformed.

Of course, it wasn't to himself alone that Cayce offered this sort of advice about finding peace. For example, just one month later he went to great lengths to help a despondent fifty-seven-year-old man who was threatening to commit suicide. On two successive days, Cayce gave readings for this individual, trying to instill the peace of Christ in him.

It was during the second reading for that man that Cayce had a direct encounter with Christ. In fact, on some rare occasions while he gave a reading, another aspect of his mind would independently have dreamlike experiences. When these happened, he would regain normal consciousness, not remembering anything he had said in the reading but vividly aware of a simultaneous dreamlike experience he had just had.

On that day in mid-May, Cayce's wife Gertrude gave the suggestion for him to awaken following the reading for this suicidal man. But instead, from the entranced state Cayce continued to speak. It had been just a month since that reading for himself had advised his being alert for direct encounters with Christ. Now as he spoke, it was happening. "Jesus of Nazareth passeth by. Let Him fill thine heart with the hopes of those promises that are indeed thine, wilt thou but apply. Trust ye in the Lord." (378-41 Reports)

Then Cayce awakened. Although he recalled nothing of what he had just said in the reading—about the troubled man or about Jesus—he told Gertrude of a powerful dream that had just come to him. "I saw the Master walking down a road toward us—*all* of us, expectant, waiting for Him to come—and He was smiling: seemed very happy."

The same promise is ours. The greatest peace imaginable comes from feeling the Presence of Christ. Do we believe it's possible? Maybe what stands in the way is our own limited idea of *how* Christ can draw close to us. We need to expand the possibilities and realize that it's not always a vision or a voice. That presence may simply come as a feeling—a gentle reminder that we are loved. Or it may come to us as an inner knowing that everything is being worked out according to a plan. We can expand our expectations and let Christ come directly into our experience in a way that uniquely fits our own needs and backgrounds.

Mini-motivator: Dedicate this day for openness to experience directly the peace of Christ. But let go of any preconceived notions of how it may come. Simply be alert and receptive.

Affirmative Approaches to Peace

> ... such activities and attitudes will bring into thy experience the greater peace. Not by "Don't do this—Don't do that! ... "
>
> 528-16

"*I'D* be at peace if only I didn't have to . . . " How often do you feel that way, finishing the sentence with some annoying responsibility or irksome person you'd like to eliminate from your life? How frequently does peace of mind seem only a step away—a step that draws the line and cuts something out of your life?

It's natural to think of peace in negative terms. It's a human tendency to expect peace as the consequence of getting rid of something. An insensitive neighbor. A chronic illness. A financial problem. These are all good candidates for a negative formula for peace, the sorts of items we assume to be obstacles to peace. Hence, getting rid of them sounds as if it would probably do the trick.

But that sort of formula is what Cayce sometimes warned against. Searching for peace with a negative approach invites disappointment. Why? Because there is no guarantee that when the trouble is removed peace will be left in its place.

That was Karen's problem. She was caught in a mistaken plan for making her life more peaceful. Certainly there were troubles. Foremost was her health crisis. For two years she had struggled with a painful debilitating skin disease called scleroderma. Sometimes it left her incapable of performing her job as a church organist and choir director.

Perhaps even more painful was her relationship with Jonathan. Several years earlier he had wanted to marry her, but she put him off, not sure that he was really the one for her. She expected him to wait on her, to give her some time to make up her mind. Then her skin disease came along, and the tentative quality of their relationship faded away. He began to date others, especially one younger, attractive woman. Now Karen wanted him. She was sure that Jonathan was the right man for her.

By the time Karen received a reading from Cayce her life was in turmoil. His advice covered both physical—recommendations and remedies for her skin problem—and spiritual aspects. Essentially she needed to find peace. But her method of finding it was really a negative approach: If only I could get rid of this scleroderma, then I'd be peaceful; if only that rival woman would disappear, then my life would be tranquil.

The best formula for her would be the same for you, in whatever troubling condition you find yourself. It involves taking a positive, affirming approach to the search for peace. Temporarily assume that *at least for a while nothing is going to go away.* Now, how will you build peace in your life in spite of those difficulties? What kind of steps can you take to create peace in your experience? Your answer to those questions points the way to peace.

Mini-motivator: Notice where in your life you've been trying to get rid of something in order to be more peaceful and content. For a few days suspend that effort. Operate under the assumption that at least for a time conditions aren't going to change. Nothing is going to go away.

Now, take some creative, positive steps to build peace in your life. Replace the negative approach to peace with an affirmative one.

Empathy

. . . put self in the other fellow's place . . . Then may the life
be the more joyous, the more at peace, the more in accord.
930-1

It had been another tormenting night; three times this
week Doug hadn't slept well. He knew why. It was all the
problems he'd been having with his suppliers. They
weren't coming through on time with the materials they
had promised. As plant manager, Doug was responsible
for doing something about it.

But why this week? He'd been in management roles
with this company for fifteen years. Problems and difficult decisions were part of the job. Yet he couldn't remember having had his sleep so disturbed in the past.
Was it because he had taken such a tough stance with
one of the tardy suppliers? He had angrily let that man
know that their contract was voided because of the
delay. Sure, he knew this would get the supplier stirred
up. But why was Doug's peace of mind eroded by
simply following hard-nosed business rules?

The next day over lunch he confided in his friend and
fellow businessman Dave Kahn. It was a bit embarrass-
ing to admit that he was losing sleep over something like
this, but Dave was a thoughtful man who might have

some good advice. Nothing would have prepared Doug for his recommendation: a business consultation from a psychic living 400 miles away. The whole process could be done through the mail, and Doug wouldn't even have to meet this man Edgar Cayce. Even though it sounded strange, he was ready to try anything to regain his peace of mind and to rest at night.

Two weeks later the materials from Cayce arrived. Four typed pages that analyzed Doug's character and business life. At first he was skeptical. Dave must have tipped Cayce off because no one could know some of this information. But as he thought more carefully, he realized that not even his friend Dave knew some of these facts about his feelings and hopes.

Cayce's most important piece of business advice focused on empathy. Doug already had the management skills to do well at his job, it stated. The only question was whether or not he had the people skills to find peace and contentment in his profession. The secret was getting inside the thinking and life experience of someone else. " . . . put self in the other fellow's place." (930-1) Then Doug would be able to see what needed to be done. Sometimes it would require being tough and hard-nosed. Other times it might mean being a little more patient and tolerant. Each situation would be different, and no management book could provide firm guidelines.

Doug was going to have to learn this new skill: being empathic. Cayce promised him a good night's sleep. He'd rest well after any day that he practiced a willingness to look at situations from the other person's point of view. Peace of mind and peace of heart were within his reach. But he was going to have to make some changes.

Mini-motivator: Every time today that you encounter a situation that upsets your peace of mind, try being empathic. Use your imagination to re-create the events from the point of view of the other person. How do you suppose he or she has experienced what's been happening? After you've done this, act on what seems fair and right for everyone involved.

Right Effort

Know in *yourself* that you are doing the right, and let the move be on the part of others . . . the mental satisfaction of knowing that ye are *trying* makes a peace that may not be had otherwise.   1183-3

NONE of us can make someone else change. But when we're in a disruptive situation that destroys our peace, we know we've got to do *something*. Janet was in one of the worst situations imaginable. Her husband was alcoholic and dependent. What made matters even worse, the lady she had taken in as a boarder was irritable and disturbing. These two people were making her life miserable, and she developed a bad case of high blood pressure.

Janet sought help from Cayce for two reasons. She knew she needed to control her hypertension. Otherwise, it might leave her vulnerable to a stroke. She realized that something had to change in her chaotic, tense home life.

Her reading from Cayce promised her the peace that she wanted so desperately. It would require that she follow a careful strategy for dealing with these issues. First, the disruptive renter had to go; she wasn't likely to change her ways. The news could be broken lovingly to the woman, but Janet had to be firm in her resolve.

The problem with her husband wouldn't be so easily handled. According to Cayce, the alcoholism was in a very advanced and serious stage. Although there was still a chance that he would get hold of his life and change, there were no guarantees. In such an impossible situation, how could Janet hope to find peace of mind? Cayce proposed a formula to her.

His recommendation goes right to the heart of human psychology. It contains advice that any of us could apply if we found ourselves in a seemingly hopeless tangle with someone. Resist the temptation to think that it's all up to you. Make peace with yourself by doing *everything* you can to help the situation—but then let go of any expectations about how conditions will turn out. If you know that you've done your very best, then it won't be hard to find an inner peace, even if situations around you are still in turmoil.

Continuing this line of reasoning, Cayce told Janet to watch her words and deeds carefully. Never do anything for which you might feel regret later. No matter what others say or do about this unfortunate situation, follow what you know is the best for you. If you're successful at this, the peace that has been promised to you is assured.

It takes great courage to follow that pathway through an emotional upheaval. Our natural human tendency is to blame—sometimes to blame the other person for the unfairness of it all; sometimes to blame ourselves for not being strong enough or wise enough to make it all turn out right. But the most reliable way to a genuine peace is to make sure each day that we've done our best and then leave the results in God's hands.

Mini-motivator: Pick one situation in your life where you've been trying to change situations and make them better. Try a new strategy—one that promises to help you maintain an inner peace. Make a commitment to do your very best in the situation, but let go of the tension that comes from thinking it's all up to you.

Sustaining World Peace

> For what preserves the equanimity of the earth today? The same as did in that illustration recorded in how Abram or Abraham pled for the cities . . . Those have held, these do hold, opportunities open for others.   877-9

SOMETIMES current events are so upsetting that you probably want to put down the newspaper or turn off the TV evening news. What's keeping the world from completely going down the tubes anyway? It seems as if everything ought to sink from the weight of pain, suffering, and selfishness.

Cayce's answer to this troubling question was to recall the Old Testament story of Abraham. Although God was ready to destroy Sodom because of its corruption, He entered into a bargain with Abraham. If a sufficient number of righteous people could be identified, that would be enough to warrant sparing the city. First the target number was forty people, but after some negotiating, the figure was lowered to just ten. Unfortunately not even ten righteous souls could be found.

Assuming that this story describes a spiritual law, just how does it work? How can a small number of people sustain relative peace and stability in the world? By what power is this possible? Is it even fair? It would appear more lawful if every person, community, and nation had to pay for its shortcomings.

Cayce's answers offer an interesting slant on these questions. It's not so much that a handful of people can *save* a city or a country. In fact, no one can override the free will or the destiny of another. If a society is intent on self-destruction, it will probably destroy itself eventually.

What a righteous group *can* do, however, is alter the tone of the situation. It can "hold opportunities open" for everyone. In other words, the consciousness and the actions of a relatively small number of enlightened people have a far-reaching impact. It's not an influence that nullifies the freedom of anyone, but it keeps options from getting closed off; it keeps the alternative for peace and righteousness available.

Sometimes this happens simply by example. Particularly in this day and age of mass media, it's possible for millions of people to know about the inspiring deeds of a small group of committed individuals. That knowledge keeps the possibility open. On other occasions, parapsychology may have the best explanation for how the influence is communicated. If we really are connected to everyone else at a subconscious level—as psychical research suggests—then the high ideals and peace-loving acts of even just a few people have a widespread effect. Through a kind of unconscious telepathy, the option for peace stays alive in every one. Admittedly, for peace to be a reality, it still requires that individuals choose that option. But an extraordinary contribution is made by those who simply keep the "opportunities open for others." (877-9)

Mini-motivator: Be an agent for peace today—peace that extends far beyond your close circle of friends and acquaintances. Try to be aware of your connections to the rest of humanity. Feel how each peaceful thought or deed helps to keep that option available to people all over the world.

Honesty

Be honest with self as you would have others be honest with thee. In that manner ye may overcome all those things that bring doubt or fear.   2509-2

HER life felt as if it were slipping away. The hopeful prospects of a fulfilling career and a happy marriage—possibilities that seemed within reach just a few years earlier—now looked more and more remote. Alice was beginning to be afraid that she might end up alone and embittered.

She was now forty-six. For nine years she had been the social companion of a kind-hearted, supportive man who had come into her life just when she had been deeply disappointed by another man. But her current friend was still married. For more than a decade he had been separated from his wife but had never taken steps to legally break the bond. Although Alice at times had intentions of speaking up and honestly confronting him about this situation, somehow she was never able to be forthright. For that matter, she wasn't even sure that she was being honest with herself or clear about what she really wanted from this relationship.

The problem with truthfulness confronted her in her workplace, too. She was employed on Capitol Hill by a member of the U.S. House of Representatives. She was a top-notch office manger with fourteen years' experience, excellent Washington connections, and the respect of many influential people in government. But for some unexplainable reason, the Congressman for whom she now worked gave her none of the responsibilities and authority she had had when she worked for another Congressman. To make matters worse, he had brought with him to the Capitol the secretary from his own law office who was an ambitious, arrogant, insecure woman. The daily office situation was becoming almost insufferable for Alice. Still she didn't speak up, she didn't honestly express her frustrations.

When she finally turned to Cayce for advice, she wanted to know why she felt misunderstood, fearful, and without any real peace in her life. The reading that came back to her contained one direct message about those problems: the need for greater honesty. If she could be truthful—first to herself and then with others—her fears would dissipate.

Why is honesty so hard for many of us? Sometimes we worry about the reactions that a candid statement will stimulate. Other times we may be embarrassed to admit our genuine feelings. Everybody wrestles to some degree with being frank and open in relationships. Of course, discretion is also important. It's foolish to blurt out everything you think or feel. Timing is critical; so, too, is skill at knowing how to word your statements.

But there's a key to honesty, and it promises to diminish fear and promote inner peace. The secret is to be honest *with oneself first.* That was Alice's mistake. She hadn't found the courage to face herself and honestly recognize what she wanted from her life. Until that happened nothing was going to change in her love relations or in her professional life.

Mini-motivator: Take ten or fifteen minutes for a sincere review of your current life situation. Write down your observations. One by one go through the most significant aspects of your life and be honest with yourself. What are you feeling? What do you want in that relationship or situation? Now start being more honest with others.

Influencing Others

Fear . . . always creates activity in the mind of those feared;
but *love* . . . brings harmony or quiet . . .   290-1

HE had been gone for four years. Now one day—out of
the blue—he appeared at her doorstep. Margaret was
flustered. A contradictory mixture of emotions welled up
in her: relief, happiness, anger, bitterness. She tried to
remain calm as she invited him in.

This was no stranger. Philip was the father of her seven
children, and for the first dozen years of their marriage
he had been the perfect husband. Then one day without
warning he had left Margaret and the family. She had to
go to work to support them, eventually becoming quite
successful as the owner of her own insurance business.
The oldest child, Sandra, had taken over many of the
mothering duties. The entire family had adapted to
Philip's absence. Now he was back.

Philip had returned with every intention of staying.
Margaret accepted him and tried to put on a normal
front for the children and the community as if nothing
had happened. But she was only pretending, and after a
while her patience wore thin. He had no plans for going
back to work himself, apparently assuming that she
would support him. Although she didn't complain, she
knew this set-up wasn't right.

Finally, after a year of putting up with the awkward arrangement, she knew she needed to find a remedy for this family problem. She thought she knew where she could get some useful advice. A year earlier she had gone with her friend Louise to witness a psychic reading from Edgar Cayce. Louise, seeking help for a physical ailment, had wanted a companion that day of the reading. So Margaret contacted Mr. Cayce and secured an appointment for her own reading. Louise went along, too, this time as the supportive one herself.

Margaret's most pressing question was whether or not she and her children were in any immediate danger from him. Clearly something was still imbalanced or unsettled in Philip. Was there a chance he would turn violent?

Cayce offered a clairvoyant view of him. His troubled soul needed a reawakening and a renewal. Margaret's attitude and behavior would be pivotal. On the one hand, she should not be condemning but, on the other hand, not pampering nor compliant. Most important of all was her attitude. If she was afraid, it would stir up fear in him. If she continually thought about all that could go wrong, it would only make him more likely to move in that direction.

This sound advice from Cayce reminds us what a strong influence we have on others, particularly family members, relatives, neighbors, and work colleagues. Especially in the case of someone who is vulnerable, our own fears can tip the balance. Troubled or confused individuals are very sensitive to the thoughts and feelings of those around them—often without being directly aware of how easily they are influenced. But this fact can also be used in a positive way. Just as our own fearful thoughts stimulate fear in others, so as much do our loving thoughts make it easier for them to find peace of mind.

Oneness in the Midst of Duality

For life and death are one, and only those who will consider the experience as one may come to understand or comprehend what peace indeed means. 1977-1

PHYSICAL life is based on duality. Light and dark. Positive- and negative-charged particles of the atom. Male and female gender distinctions. Liberal and conservative political differences. The list goes on and on. In fact, we come to expect polarity in everything we encounter.

Duality gives life its tension. At its best that entails a creative, dynamic interplay that moves us along the path of growth. But more often than not, the tension of duality paralyzes us. Peace is destroyed as we feel pulled apart by competing demands. For example, it's a rare person who would experience peace in trying to reconcile the masculine and feminine aspects of self—whether in love relationships or in the inner alchemy of meeting one's own opposite sex characteristics.

Nowhere, however, is the threat to personal peace more evident than in the most fundamental duality of human existence: *the polarity of life and death.* The stark reality of physical death is an unavoidable matter for all of us. It's an issue for even the most healthy, life-affirming person. Consciously or unconsciously, our peace of mind is eroded by the inevitability of our own impending death.

What's to be done, then, if we want to attain peace in a world of polar opposites? Is peace an unachievable ideal in this world of duality? Perhaps we can bring a *spiritual* understanding to a *physical* law. The physical world, yes, operates by duality. We're also beings of spirit. This reality makes it feasible for us to reconcile and integrate opposites. For example, it's possible to experience oneself as a soul and harmoniously blend the qualities of masculine and feminine. Even more fundamentally, from the spiritual perspective we can see that earthly life and death are two sides of the same coin.

Only those who consider life and death as a oneness will be able to understand what peace means. That basic principle came from Cayce in response to the needs of a New York City jail inmate. In fact, before giving the reading, Cayce went to visit the man in prison. He wasn't a hardened killer who was facing the death penalty. He wasn't facing the realities of life and death any more directly than millions of people do every day. He was simply a man who had made some mistakes in a difficult world where peace is hard to find.

The man was determined to turn his life around. The district attorney was inclined to offer him another chance. Cayce's advice in the reading gave him a guiding principle: Keep looking for the continuity of life. Try to see the tension-producing dualities from the angle of your spiritual self. Peace will be yours when you can see the underlying oneness.

Mini-motivator: Pick one of the many polar tensions of physical life that may be upsetting your peace of mind. For example, it could be worries about death, troubles in a love relation, or contrary points of view with a work associate. Try for a day to see the issue from the perspective of your spiritual self—a point of view that operates from oneness.

Avoiding Offense

> . . . it was necessary that offenses come but that the self should not be offended nor offend others, and with such an attitude one will indeed eventually find peace in self.
>
> 3342-1

PEOPLE who are thin-skinned find it hard to be at peace. Slights, slurs, rudeness—these are the ingredients of fast-paced, tension-filled modern life. Anyone who is quick to take offense will find plenty about which to get upset.

It's not enough that we feel hurt and offended at the time the affront occurs. When we're mistreated, we also tend to hang on to the memory. We keep track of who uses us—a kind of mental ledger in which accounts are kept. The disruption to our peace of mind, therefore, extends for days or weeks afterward.

What can you do personally to minimize this disturbing human trait? How can you learn to avoid taking offense when you're treated badly? The first step is to remember that more often than not the offending party doesn't really have you personally in mind as a target. You haven't been singled out in a premeditated, purposeful way. That individual is unhappy and simply takes it out on the surrounding world. The person wants to share his or her misery, and unfortunately you happened to get in the way. Of course, realizing that you weren't the intended target doesn't erase the annoyance or the trouble. But it can make it a little easier to let go of any resentful memory.

Another strategy is to refuse to take the offense. Just as you can refuse a C.O.D. package or a collect phone call, you can decline the wound it may give to your self-esteem. You may not be able to stop the behavior itself, but you have control over the mood it creates in you. No doubt you've experienced the difference between an irritating action and the subjective feeling of being offended. If a toddler spits up on you, you probably won't like it, but you're not going to feel offended.

It's just one more step to being able to control your own reactions to rude and thoughtless behavior. You don't have to like the way you've been treated—and may even need to communicate firmly your displeasure—but you can choose not to take it as a personal offense that destroys your peace of mind.

In fact, this capacity to rise above hurt feelings has long been recognized as a secret to peace. Apparently it's not just the modern world that's filled with insensitive people. As the Old Testament psalmist put it: "Great peace have they which love thy law: and nothing shall offend them." (Psalm 119:165 KJV)

Mini-motivator: For one day make this commitment to yourself: I won't take offense at any mistreatment or slight that I receive from someone. I don't have to like everything that comes my way—I may need to speak up about something—but I won't let any slight, slur, or annoyance undermine my peace.

Creating Peace

Remember, ye pursue peace, ye embrace peace, ye hold to peace. It is not something that descends upon thee, save as ye *have* created and do create it in the hearts, in the minds, in the experiences of others.   3051-2

W_{HEN} we're tired and hassled, we'd love to have peace descend on us like a dove from heaven. It's easy to imagine that sort of magical intervention. Like a troubled child whose parent steps in to save it, peace would simply be there.

The problem is that's not the way life operates. Peace is ours, but we've got to create it—or, perhaps more accurately put, *cocreate* it with God. Peace is a byproduct of our efforts. It requires us to take an *active* stance in the world.

In fact, peace is a lot like patience. Both are frequently understood—or misunderstood—to be exclusively a passive relationship with the surrounding world. For example, when we're told to be patient, what's really the message? Be willing to wait. Passively put up with what's going on, and after a while conditions will change.

But to understand fully either patience or peace we need to see its active side, too. Active patience is first of all an inner process, a careful attention to one's attitudes and feelings. For instance, standing in line for an hour without complaining isn't really patience if one is inwardly stewing with frustration. But, of course, active patience also has an outer element. The truly patient person doesn't merely sit back and wait for changes to happen. That individual gets involved and works unhurriedly for something new.

So what would *active peace* look like? First, it's an attitude, a recognition that harmony won't supernaturally materialize all by itself. We're going to have to *do something* to help them come forth.

Second, it's a willingness to get involved in the lives of others in a purposeful way. There's a *social dimension* to active peace. As we help others to experience peace in their own lives, it comes alive in our own as well. To many people this is a rather radical idea. The more familiar image of peace entails getting away from people—finding some peace and quiet by oneself. Even though there's certainly a need for times alone, the idea of active peace turns the conventional theory upside down—it claims there's another side to the story. Instead of passivity, it means activity. Rather than Spartan, it encourages involvement. Maybe up until now we've been looking for peace with only half the picture in mind.

Mini-motivator: Take an active stance today for peace. Look for situations in which you can take steps to build peace, especially for opportunities to help other people experience it.

Children of Peace

And if you commit that peace to thy son, he — too — may put his hand in the hand of the Master . . .   3165-1

THESE words from Edgar Cayce had a powerful effect on Carolyn. For several years she had been increasingly concerned about her son Jeffrey. He seemed to be an overly sensitive child, with a slight stammer and a problem with bed-wetting. He was overly attached to her, constantly clinging to her, and seemed unable to enjoy being with other people. In so many ways he appeared to be underdeveloped, as if he were eight or nine years old instead of his real age, eleven.

Carolyn worried that she was the cause of these difficulties. While she was pregnant with him, many situations in her life made her extremely unhappy. Could her depression have been transmitted to Jeffrey in such a way that his development was retarded slightly? Or was it something she was doing *now* that was continuing to contribute to the problem?

Cayce's reading was for Jeffrey, but many of the comments and suggestions were directed toward Carolyn. He confirmed that Jeffrey was born with certain emotional disturbances and that his mother's emotional state had had an impact. But all that was in the past.

There was no use in feeling guilty when many positive things could be done right now to assist him.

First, Cayce recommended that Carolyn adopt greater peace of mind about his slow development. He would catch up. In their own timing, the changes would come naturally.

Next, the reading described the kind of parental support that would help Jeffrey experience greater peace and security himself. Just as Carolyn's prenatal emotions influenced her son, even eleven years later there was still a connection. If she would clarify her own ideals and beliefs, it would subtly affect him. If she would focus and commit her energies to high values and purposes, it would boost Jeffrey's ability to start doing the same for his own life. Most of all, Carolyn could be an influence for peace in the life of her son. In doing so, it would enable him, as he grew older, to build a stronger and stronger relationship to Christ.

Teaching peace to our children is a potent message. We live in a world that continually bemoans the academic skills of our youth, that criticizes their social habits, and worries about their lack of commitment to high values. But what have we taught them about peace? Rather than blame teachers, television, or video games, we'd do better to examine our own influence on them. We all have children in our lives—whether we're parents, grandparents, aunts, uncles, or next-door neighbors. We all have a responsibility to teach peace to the younger generation.

Mini-motivator: Make a focused effort to be a teacher of peace to one child in your life. First of all, by your example demonstrate what living peacefully looks like. In addition, try to find ways that you can promote peace of mind for that child, as well as peaceful relationships with friends and family.

Opposing Fear

For fear is—as it ever has been—that influence that
opposes will, and yet fear is only of the moment while will
is of eternity.   1210-1

TED had worked hard to become successful in his career as a physician—college, medical school, and then
years gaining his reputation as a first-class doctor. But
when he reached his early 50s, everything started to
change. He lost interest in medicine and quit, and his
marriage began to come apart. It was at that point that a
friend in New York told him about Cayce, and Ted de-
cided to request a reading about his life's purpose.

"Should I go back to medical practice?" he asked. Not
full time, was Cayce's advice. You need more freedom in
your life's path. In fact, freedom is the key to understanding your mission in this lifetime.

The reading told a detailed story of his soul's purpose—for this current lifetime and for the preceding one
in which he had also worked as a physician. During the
Revolutionary War he "looked after the health as related
to cleanliness about the encampments . . . " (1210-1) But
his constant goal was more than preventing infections
and healing wounds. It was also freedom. This meant the
cause of the colonists fighting British oppression; and it

also meant *freedom from fear.*

So strong was this commitment that it carried over into his twentieth-century lifetime. He had come with powerful urges to promote freedom, especially to help other people break loose from anything that would bind them. In particular, his calling was to assist individuals to be free of their fears. Cayce even summarized this mission for Ted in a succinct statement of his soul's purpose: " . . . to *free souls* from fear!!" (1210-1)

That's a noble undertaking. How does one do it? How do we get rid of our own fears, let alone help someone else do it? Cayce's recommendations to this fifty-four-year-old man included one important clue: Awaken your free will. Recognize that any fear is the opposite of will—it is the antithesis of freedom. If you've surrendered your will and you're letting other people or outside events control your life, then you're bound to be fearful.

That clue can lead us to a remarkable discovery: Something extraordinary happens when we use free will and *act*, even in the face of fear. By doing something—rather than being paralyzed—our sense of time is altered. What dawns on us is that fear is only momentary—the situation or person that scares us is temporary. But something else is timeless. That other ingredient that comes clearly into focus is the will—that is, our freedom and our individuality. We experience our own timelessness and our own place in eternity.

Mini-motivator: The next time you're anxious or afraid, use this affirmation: "This fear is only momentary—my real self is eternal." Use the words to help you get in touch with the continuity of life, your own immortality. Then *act* in the situation. Do something—the best that you know to do. Use your will, knowing that free will is the opposite of fear.

PART THREE

FREE YOURSELF TO
LOVE UNCONDITIONALLY

Know that the power of thyself is very limited. The power of Creative Force is unlimited.   2981-1

Introduction

A loving relationship is like no other interaction. It doesn't come with a guarantee or warranty. Authentic love isn't based on conditions or stipulations: it's *unconditional*.

That kind of loving sounds like scary business. It's risky because it doesn't come with any assurances. We never know when we're likely to be disappointed, rejected, or hurt by someone. Once we remove the preconditions and simply love, we're vulnerable. So, why do the greatest spiritual teachings always challenge us to reach for that kind of unconditional love?

The answer is that unconditional love *does*, in fact, come with an assurance. But the promise isn't that the person we love will necessarily reciprocate. Sometimes that individual is too wounded or filled with self-doubt to be capable of immediately giving back love. No, the assurance that we're offered points to another type of reward. The act of loving, without any requirements or expectations, fills us with indescribable joy and creative energy. When we love this way, we catch a glimpse of how God loves us.

Being convinced that the risk is worth the potential reward isn't enough. The trick is to be *able* to love unconditionally. We're caught up in our fears and insecurities, which make selfless love appear beyond our reach. Our illusions and mistaken notions of how life works create a formidable barrier. What we've got to do first is *free ourselves*—free ourselves so that we can love unconditionally.

Tolerance

So few souls or entities have combined love in the material plane with tolerance! For, love in the material becomes egotistical, and this is opposite from tolerance.   2629-1

MICHELLE had something going for her. She had a special quality about her and people could feel it. Her warmth and supportive insights touched people every day. She was well placed in her vocation as a school counselor working with adolescents.

Edgar Cayce could clairvoyantly see this remarkable quality in her character, though he never met her personally. In fact, Michelle's reading contains one of the finest compliments Cayce ever gave: " . . . God so loved the world as to give His only begotten Son. So has this entity so loved its fellow man as to give itself, its life, its abilities, its virtues, that others might know—too—that God is mindful of them." (2629-1)

What, exactly, was it that made her so special? Most simply, it was tolerance. This elusive quality was hard to find in Edgar Cayce's time; probably, even harder today. How infrequently we give other people the benefit of the doubt! How seldom we "cut someone a little slack," as the saying goes!

Maybe what makes tolerance so rare is that it seems

illogical. With minds that are usually alert for faults and inconsistencies, we're inclined to pounce on the shortcomings of competitors and strangers, not to mention family, friends, and colleagues. To be tolerant means to be willing to dismiss something that appears to us to be obviously wrong.

The psychology of *in*tolerance goes something like this: Since life usually seems to keep our own noses close to the grindstone, why not require that same sort of accountability from others? Since it often feels as if parents, spouses, or bosses keep us on short leashes, why not react to other people's errors? It wouldn't make sense to do otherwise, would it?

In fact, tolerance—and love itself, for that matter—often entails being rather illogical. Many of the applications of Jesus' parables about love aren't very rational if we try to use modern-day common sense. Who'd be tolerant of a pushy person who demands your coat? Who'd be so illogical—that is, so loving—as to offer the outer cloak as well?

Tolerance requires a certain *flexibility of spirit.* It allows conditions to keep going, even when someone hasn't exactly measured up to what he or she ought to be or even *could* be with a little more effort. Think about this example in terms of how the word is used in mechanical engineering. Tolerance is the measure of how much deviation is acceptable. In the manufacturing of a door and its frame, the cuts might have a tolerance of one-eighth inch. As long as the production errors are no larger, the door will operate smoothly. But to exceed that tolerance level invites problems.

The same process goes on in human relations. Unfortunately, caring doesn't necessarily go hand-in-hand with being tolerant. If Cayce is correct about our material-world experience, our loving concern easily becomes "egotistical." In other words, we tend to allow biases, personal expectations, and rigidity to make us intolerant.

Michelle's quality of tolerance is a beautiful example for us all. Just imagine what she was dealing with every day in her work with adolescents! Teenagers are always testing our limits. They're experimenting with options, so it's easy for adults to be judgmental. But in the midst of that sort of daily vocational challenge, she found a way to remember the divine spark in everyone.

She was able to overlook differences and shortcomings, not out of naiveté or blindness, but because she could also see something else about each person.

Mini-motivator: Try one day to be especially tolerant. When someone makes an error or exhibits a fault, suspend your reaction. Even if it seems illogical to let these shortcomings pass without a word of criticism or judgment, allow the relationship to keep working because of your loving flexibility.

Overcoming Self-Doubt

(Q) Why is it so hard for me to "give out" in love and appreciation?
(A) . . . unless ye measure up within yourself, ye have nothing to give. 3691-1

SELF-doubt paralyzes the human soul. As much as any other attitude or emotion, it blocks us from freely loving. Self-doubt freezes the heart and uses up the vital energy we need in order to warmly embrace the life around us.

We all have times when we doubt ourselves. It's hard to imagine being human without periods of it. Apparently even Jesus had moments in which He wasn't sure He was up to what was asked of Him. These are times of testing. The self-doubt may only be temporary as we get up the courage to step forward boldly and meet our destiny.

But these natural and fairly short-lived events can sometimes turn into something far darker. For some individuals disbelief in one's own adequacy can turn into a frightful trap from which no escape seems possible.

Amanda was caught in the depths of chronic self-doubt. Her home life was so painful and strained that she felt inadequate as a mother and wife. Her apprehension centered around her eleven-year-old daughter who was troubled with seizures. These seizures seemed to have begun about the time Amanda's second child was born. From the time of his birth, this son had seemed very special to her. How was it possible for a parent to favor one child over another, she wondered? But undeniably she did have warmer feelings for her son than she did for her daughter. In her heart she knew that her daughter sensed it and felt left out. She worried guiltily that the seizures were a result of the daughter feeling disfavored.

Her self-doubts took her to such a low that, by her own admission, turning to Cayce for a reading was her last resort. "What's wrong with me?" she wanted to know. "Why can't I love the way I know I should?"

Cayce immediately put one aspect of her worries at rest. The daughter's seizures were not the result of her mother's behavior or feeling. It was a deep karmic issue within the soul of the daughter. She had come to this family to work on the problem, but it was not the byproduct of Amanda's favoritism.

At first it may look as if she were being let off the hook, so to speak, by Cayce's clairvoyant view of the family dynamics. The seizures had a cause of their own. But Cayce went on to remind her of a change that *was* her responsibility: In order to love, you've got to "measure up within yourself." (3691-1)

Honing in on the real problem for Amanda, Cayce identified an inward quality, a feeling of falling short. Here was the cause of her dark self-doubts. He counseled her: It's not so much a question of failing to do what you ought to do. Sure, there are times when you don't act the way you know you should. But remember, loving action will come as a natural result when your inner life is straightened out. First, you've got to "measure up within yourself." (3691-1) In other words, your self-esteem needs a boost. When you take a measure on yourself, you need to discover that you really do stand tall. "Believe in yourself, Amanda"—that's the heart of Cayce's advice. Even though you're not perfect yet, the core of your being is good, worthy, and loving. When you stay in touch with that feeling, self-doubts dissipate, and you'll be able to meet lovingly the ambiguities and the struggles that your family faces.

Mini-motivator: Take five minutes some time today for taking a measure on yourself. But let that time be something other than a review of your shortcomings. Feel any self-doubts fade away as you focus on what's right and good about yourself. "Stand tall" in your own estimation. Then, after those five minutes of affirmation, see if it comes naturally for you to be loving to those around you.

Gifts from the Unpretentious

... it is not in the thunder or lightning, it is not in the storm, it is not in the loudness—but the still small voice within! So as ye write, so as ye talk, so as ye love—let it be in meekness of spirit... 1472-3

MARIE was having an awful day at work. She had been feeling ill since she arrived at her office early that morning. But as a radio broadcaster in New York City in the late 1930s, she had a very responsible job, and it wasn't easy to take a day off.

In her office that day an astounding healing took place. Here, in the midtown Manhattan hub of communications and powerful influence, something unexpected came into Marie's life. It was a quiet, meek, unpretentious presence that brought healing. So dramatic was the event for her that she wrote about in a letter to her friend Edgar Cayce.

" ... I was sitting at my desk in my office. A deaf-mute lad somehow got past everyone in the reception room and came into my office. He handed me a card saying he was deaf and dumb, and asking that I buy some scratch pads he was selling to make a living. I bought the pads, paid the young man (he was about sixteen), laid the pads on my desk, and turned with a sigh to my work for I was feeling very ill indeed that day. I thought no more about the boy until suddenly I looked up. He had reached the door, turned and looked at me, and with a smile returned to my desk, took a pencil, and wrote these words on one of the scratch pads I had bought:

"BE WELL!

"And instantly I was well.

"Furthermore, I believe the Christ was in my office that morning—made manifest through this dear afflicted child who could not heal himself, but who left the Christ with me in healing blessing."

How often do we remember to look for the greatest in the smallest? In the busyness of our daily schedules, in our preoccupation with what we assume is important, how frequently do we pause to recognize God's presence in the modest and meek aspects of life? Certainly, healing love can come from a still, small voice that is *internal*. But perhaps just as often it's likely to come to us *externally*—via other people. More often than not, it's the humble and unpretentious individuals who have the most to offer.

Mini-motivator: Be ready today to receive gifts from God that come to you via unassuming, unpretentious people whom you encounter. Pay attention to what these individuals have to say and to what they demonstrate by their actions.

Making Freedom a Priority

Choose the freedom, rather than money. It will make for more harmonious conditions; though there may be periods when anxieties will arise. But freedom is worth it all.

989-2

BETH felt as if she were at a crossroads. She was thirty-one, as yet unmarried, and with a budding career as a stage performer. Was she missing out on what would make her happy in the long run—a home, a husband, and a family? There wasn't much time to waste if she were going to pursue that path.

But her heart right now was in her career, a profession that was risky. As a performer, she could never be sure what lay just ahead. Oftentimes, there were temptations: chances to let money be the top priority in the type of work she accepted.

In the midst of this quandary, Beth's mother recommended that she turn to Edgar Cayce for advice. Her mother had previously received useful counsel from a reading, and the daughter's situation looked like just the type that could use a fresh perspective.

Beth's reading from Cayce was direct. Go with your career. Marriage is not for you; in fact, it would be a hardship. The confinement and restriction you'd be likely to find in a marriage would overpower and overwhelm you. Your rather obstinate nature would make such a daily relationship difficult for you and your partner.

It's easy to imagine that this advice was a bit deflating to Beth when she first read it. To be told that you're unsuited for marriage could easily diminish one's self-esteem. But Beth's reading gave her a much larger view of her purpose in life. It not only cautioned against a permanent love relation, it also pointed her in the direction where she *was* most likely to find fulfillment.

Cayce went on to tell Beth that she was certainly capable of love, but that for her *freedom* was the key. Instead of being tied down to marriage and family, her soul sought to give and to express love to others through her profession. It promised that she would be successful and happy if she would make freedom a priority in her planning. There would be times when she might feel the allure of money and the security it would offer. But the love she had to offer the world through her performing career would thrive only if she maintained her freedom.

Mini-motivator: Within the context of the responsibilities you've accepted for your life right now, make freedom a priority for one day. For example, avoid overcommitting yourself. Or don't make decisions which might promise financial benefits but are likely to restrict your freedom.

Love and Talents

One . . . may use [abilities] to entice, overpower, to subdue,
to subjugate others *to* the power, unless guided, directed,
and *loved into* the correct idea of the use of power . . .

                                                    38-1

Jo was quite a child. Anyone who was around her for
even a short time could tell that there was something
special about this girl. Clearly she was talented—what's
sometimes called a "gifted child." Jo's parents knew that
they had a big responsibility to help channel all that potential so that she would mature into a creative, healthy
young woman.

They turned to Edgar Cayce for suggestions. Jo's father
had good reason to believe that psychic advice could be
helpful. Several times the Cayce source had made a big
difference in his own life. Recommendations about his
nausea and indigestion had helped him overcome those
ailments. Business problems in his interior-design profession had been solved by following Cayce's psychic
counsel. Now it was time to see what sort of child-rear-
ing principles would help them with Jo.

The message they heard about their daughter was essentially this: Love her into what's best for her; that is,
don't order or command her to use her talents and skills

in the way you think she should, but love her into the right use of her powers.

Cayce went on to say that Jo is a child given to extremes. Her exceptional abilities—especially in the arts—could make her vulnerable to wild swings from one extreme to the other. Extraordinary good can potentially come out of her life or "exceptional abilities to err, or to be led astray . . . " (38-1) Nothing would be more valuable to Jo than to have caring family members who would simply love her into fulfilling her positive potential.

That's sound advice to *any* parent. In fact, every child is gifted in some way or another. Even though many children may not have Jo's propensity to go astray in the use of her talents, a parent could hardly go wrong by replacing coercion or authoritarian direction with loving support.

But Cayce's principle here has even wider applicability. Often we see talented friends, neighbors, and work colleagues apparently misusing their talents. Any talent or ability is really a power, and that power can be misdirected to "entice, overpower, to subdue, to subjugate others . . . " (38-1) Does it do any good to command others to straighten out and use those talents more productively? Does it work to logically reason with them? Rarely—if ever.

What works is to "love them into" wiser use of their abilities. Love builds self-esteem. Unconditional support frees others to use their powers in a new way.

Mini-motivator: We all attempt to influence others. It's a natural part of human relations. But for two or three days give up trying to "talk people into" doing specific actions or "reasoning them into" following a certain path. Instead put that same energy into simply loving and supporting them. Try "loving them into" their best.

Preferring Others

And in *love* show the *preference* for that *companionship*, in
the *little things* that make the larger life the bigger and the
better!   903-3

W HAT do you prefer? That's the sort of choice we face
each day in many little ways; for example, picking a flavor of ice cream or choosing which brand of soup to buy
at the grocery store. Or selecting one channel over another when sitting down to watch the evening news.

But those are commonplace, mundane examples.
Preference has a deeper meaning, too. It implies value—
even love. What you prefer is that to which you give energy and attention. It's what you love, so to speak.
Nowhere is this clearer than in the challenge to prefer
someone else and his or her needs, even over your own.

Cayce's frequent advice was to show love by preferring
the other. An ancient Jewish folk tale illustrates this won-
derfully.

There were once two brothers who labored each day
in a common field. Life wasn't easy for them, but they
felt blessed to have a way to sustain themselves. The elder had never married, but the younger had a wife and
three small children.

When autumn came and the harvest was brought in,

they divided the fruits of their labors in half. It had always been their custom to divide the grain fifty-fifty. Each took his share to his own storage barn. Some of the grain would be sold and the money used for other necessities. The rest of the food would be slowly consumed in the months ahead.

But shortly after the grain had been divided this year, the older brother had trouble sleeping. Something didn't seem right to him about the method they were using. He thought to himself, "My brother has a wife and children. His needs are greater than mine. He should have gotten a bigger portion than I." So, in the middle of the night, he secretly carried sacks of his grain to his brother's home and left them outside behind the barn.

Somewhat later that same night, the younger brother also had trouble sleeping. He, too, felt that something wasn't right about the way the grain had been allocated. He reasoned, "My brother has no family. I have children who will care for me and for my wife when we are old, but he has none. A greater portion of the grain should go to him each year so that he can sell it and save the money for his old age." So the younger brother got up and, taking sacks of grain from inside his barn, he traveled secretively across the field and unloaded them behind his brother's barn.

The next morning each brother was surprised to find sacks of grain behind his respective barn. It seemed like a miracle. Each had given away some of his own portion during the night, only to find that some mysterious source, it seemed, had replaced it.

The following night both the elder and the younger brother repeated their deeds. Again, the morning brought amazement.

But on the third night, as both brothers continued their efforts to redivide the harvest, they happened to meet under the moonlit sky in the middle of their field. Then they realized what a miracle it had really been! Out of love, *each had preferred the other over himself.* Even though neither was any the richer with money or grain for these nightly trade-offs, both were profoundly enriched with love.

Mini-motivator: Pick one person in your life with whom you have frequent interactions. Then for even just a single day try as often as possible to prefer him or her over yourself—that is, put that individual's needs before your own.

Knowing Self

(Q) Need I fear loving any man, or must I be calculating?
(A) When self has found self, such relationships are the
natural inspiration of the spiritual.   911-5

JANE'S story is one of the most tragic to be found in the
Cayce files. Although we'd rather learn from the successes—people whose lives were straightened out or
healed by following Cayce's suggestions—this one
doesn't have a happy ending.

Jane and her husband were mismatched. She was the
twenty-four-year-old wife of an attorney, who was
eleven years older than she. But it would contradict
Cayce's most important piece of advice to blame her serious problems on him or on their relationship. Things
weren't right *within herself.* Jane wasn't going to have a
happy relationship with any man until she knew herself
better and loved herself.

The root of her dissatisfaction—what drove her to
seek help from Cayce—was an unfulfilled sex life. On the
one hand, she claimed her husband was "unmasculine
and abnormal sexually." On the other hand, he claimed
she was oversexed. The marriage was coming apart. Jane
even wondered if having sexual relations outside of mar-

riage would be a good idea.

One gets the immediate impression from her questions to Cayce that she was already thinking about what would come next for her. Looking for another man, how could she avoid making a similar mistake? Should she fear commitments that might lead to something like this again? Should she be shrewd and calculating, finding out secrets about a man before getting too involved?

Cayce recommended a separation. His clairvoyant view was that her husband really did have a problem with sexuality, one that had physical causes. The marital difficulty was *not* his lack of care for her. Nevertheless, a parting appeared to be best for both of them. Sadly, Jane was never able to overcome her deep sense of failure and unhappiness. She took her own life at the age of thirty.

Although few of us reach the depths of such despair as Jane's, there's still a powerful lesson in Cayce's response to her questions. When it comes to building love relations, just how much do we have to fear? Just how clever should we be? His answer is simple, though not often easy to apply: Know yourself first. Create a solid foundation within yourself, one that's based on self-esteem and healthy self-love. Then you can well expect that balanced, fulfilling love relations are going to unfold naturally.

Mini-motivator: For the next three days try to spend at least fifteen to thirty minutes daily getting to know yourself better. For example, it could include writing down your thoughts and feelings in a journal. Or it could mean studying your recent dreams, looking for insights about forgotten sides of yourself.

Love of Good

... love good, love honor, love patience. For divine love
may bring the knowledge, the understanding, the wisdom
for the activities to bring the self in accord with Creative
Forces.   1215-4

EVERY parent's secret fear had become a reality for Thomas and Virginia. Their child had been seriously injured.
A diving accident had left Tim's sixteen-year-old body
traumatized. At first the doctors had held out little hope
that he would even survive. But Tim had always been a
headstrong fellow and his powerful will seemed to shine
through as he slowly improved. But in spite of some remarkable progress, he was still left paralyzed—probably
for life.

Thomas and Virginia's initial requests for help from
Edgar Cayce were strictly medical. Unwilling to accept
the doctors' prognosis, they hoped that clairvoyant insight would lead to some nontraditional remedy to restore his body. When those first three readings didn't get
the results for which they desperately hoped, they
turned back to Cayce for another kind of reading: one
that would restore Tim's spirits.

Apparently it worked. In a feedback letter to Mr.
Cayce, Thomas and Virginia reported that the life read-

ing had turned their son around. It had shown him a way to view his own pain and disability with greater purpose. It had taught him something invaluable about the meaning of life and how he should approach the years ahead.

Avoiding any implication of punishment, Cayce told Tim that his paralysis offered him a chance to transform a troubled spot within his soul. As a Roman soldier in a former life, he had repeatedly watched torture and persecution, and had made light of the suffering. There was now an opportunity to meet that soul memory and to transform it. He could good-naturedly make light of his *own* suffering whenever anyone felt sorry for him.

Just as important, his reading from Cayce taught him a lesson about love. Although we usually think of love as being directed toward another person, Tim was encouraged to love *qualities*. " . . . *love* good, love honor, love patience." (1215-4) In other words, it's possible for any of us to become at-one with a spiritual quality. We can value it so deeply and give ourselves to it so fully that we *become* it.

For Tim it was three qualities in particular that he needed to learn how to love. For any of us the list might well be different. But this kind of love relation—not person-to-person, but person-to-quality—is an important part of what we're all here to learn

Mini-motivator: Pick one spiritual principle and devote loving attention to it. The quality you select might be truth, freedom, kindness, peace, or any other one you deeply respect.

Take a few minutes each day to meditate quietly on that word and to feel its living presence in you. Also, watch for that quality in other people. When you notice it in others, it will help it come alive in you as well.

Varieties of Love

. . . there is loving—yet in the one it might be truly called loving indifference, while in the other it is love that is truly a creative, growing experience . . .   1472-13

MARIE was racked by guilt. She considered herself a loving, generous member of her extended family, but secretly within her heart she felt badly. She was unable to muster the same feelings of love for her granddaughter that she had for her grandson. There was no apparent reason. The children were equally special and both obviously cared deeply for their grandmother.

Marie worried that there was something wrong with herself. From where did this irrational bias originate? She turned to Edgar Cayce, hoping that he could help her troubled spirit as he had with other readings previously.

Cayce's words were reassuring. Basically he said it's okay to love people in different ways. It's natural. But in this case there is an explanation. Your relationship with these two souls goes far back in time. You knew them both in one previous lifetime thousands of years ago. The soul who is now the granddaughter was in that distant time period a very independent sort of person, neither needing nor asking for much supportive help. In the

present, you genuinely care for her, but it's a less involved kind of love—a loving indifference that trusts that
her life is unfolding just as it should.

On the other hand, centuries ago you had a very different type of relationship with the soul that is now your
grandson. There was a bond forged because he often
sought your counsel, help, and instruction. So it's quite
natural that your love for him now would continue to be
very involved in and concerned for his welfare. The loving sense of responsibility has carried over.

This angle on loving should be useful to all of us. When
we examine closely our feelings about the people we
love, we're bound to discover differences. The cause of
those variations won't always involve reincarnation. But
let's keep in mind that past lives were only a secondary
part of Cayce's message to Marie anyway. The most important aspect of his advice was simply that it's okay to
love people in different ways. Just as no two souls are
identical, our loving feelings toward two individuals are
sure to have distinctions. Part of what makes life rich and
interesting is variety—even variety in how we experience
love.

Mini-motivator: Take an inventory of your love relations. Recognize variations in how you feel. Then give
yourself the freedom to be loving in different ways to different people.

Competing Loves

The influence or force that motivates the life of each soul
is love! But it may be love of self, of fame, of fortune, of
glory, of beauty, or of self-indulgence, self-aggrandizement, or the satisfaction to the ego!   1579-1

JEAN'S life was a whirlwind of one crisis after another.
After a painful divorce from Tony, she had begun to have
second thoughts about losing him. She told him that she
might be interested in a reconciliation. But before they
could arrange a time and place to meet, Jean had a serious car accident and was injured.

The meeting with Tony never got rescheduled. Apparently it would have been a waste of time anyway because
later Jean found out that he had already started up a ro-
mance with her best friend.

Not long thereafter, Jean met and fell in love with Peter. They married and moved to New York City, but it was
still the Depression Era and finances were very tight. She
was still hoping to get money in a legal settlement over
the traffic accident, but that was far from certain. To
make matters worse, her father was fired from his postal
job over a scandal of some missing money. Because he
was so depressed, Jean was worried that he might commit suicide. She wanted to move her mother and father
to New York where she could better take care of them,

but she had no idea how she could afford to do this.

Her life felt as if it were coming apart. Seemingly pulled in many different directions, she wrote to Edgar Cayce for advice. She knew of him through a family friend, a woman who had generously paid off the debt of missing postal money and saved Jean's father from the courts.

The reading came none too soon for her. The counsel from Cayce asked her to think more carefully about love. You're a loving person, it said, there's no doubt about that. You're easily able to invest your time, money, energy, and attention. But invest it in *what,* and for what *purpose?* Life gives you options. Will you merely love fortune, fame, or even just yourself? Or will you take the opportunity to love—to invest in—something bigger than yourself?

Jean's love was scattered. She was too invested in too many things in too many competing directions. The essence of Cayce's advice to her was a principle that is probably equally valid for each of us today: When your life is in disarray, it's often a problem of mixed-up loving.

Mini-motivator: Take a close look at what you've been loving. Carefully consider your priorities and the way you've been spending your energy and talents. Then establish a priority for yourself. Above all else, what do you want to love? Now spend this very day focused that way.

Love Is Letting Go

(Q) Does he [my deceased husband] know of my prayers?
(A) Do you wish him to? Do you wish to call him back
... or do you wish the self to be poured out for him that he
may be happy?   1786-2

ALL of Caroline's dreams had been dashed. It seemed
only yesterday that she was getting married and felt such
a wonderful sense of promise and hope about her life.
Bob's death after only a dozen years of marriage had stag-
gered her, as it would most anyone who loses a spouse
so early in life.

Now, two years later, she was still feeling deeply sad
and alone. She had worked occasionally as a secretary
and as a publicity writer in New York, but now she was
unemployed. But more than anything else, she missed
her husband. She prayed for him nightly and wondered
if his departed soul was still with her.

Mostly she wanted reassurance; and when she heard
of the work of Edgar Cayce, she thought that maybe he
could help. But money was a problem. How would she
ever be able to pay for a reading?

Edgar's son Hugh Lynn was in New York for extended
periods because of his work hosting a weekly radio show
called "Mysteries of the Mind." She got in touch with

Hugh Lynn and arranged a barter: She'd provide secretarial service for him in exchange for help from his father.

Naturally, she asked for psychic counsel about the relationship with her deceased husband. She wondered first if he had been trying to contact her; then, if he felt her prayers. The response from Cayce may not have been what she was hoping to hear: It's time to let go. There was much that was good from that relationship, he said—much that can be seen as soul development—but what's needed now is to release him and move on. What's best for him *and* for you is to let go of the compulsive desire to draw him back to you.

That's probably sound advice to any of us who still grieve for a loved one who has passed on. Our prayers are felt but, as much as possible, they should be prayers of blessing and release rather than attachment.

But the theme of Cayce's advice is still applicable, even if you're not presently grieving over a loved one's death. It isn't just family members and friends who die and whose memory tugs at us. There are forms of death besides physical demise. Friendships die, jobs end, phases of life conclude. Oftentimes something in us tries to hold on. We replay the memories in our imagination. We long for the "good old days." We try to re-create the past even though something new and different is really what's needed now.

Sometimes love means letting go. It can be a matter of releasing another soul to a greater life beyond—*or* simply freeing ourselves to experience fully what life has for us next.

Mini-motivator: What's something from your past that still has a powerful attraction to you—something that's clearly done with and over but which still tugs at you? For example, it may be a romantic relationship, a once rewarding job, or a wonderful period in your life.

FREE CATALOG OF BOOKS AND MEMBERSHIP ACTIVITIES

Fill-in and mail this postage-paid card today.

Please write clearly

Name: _____

Address: _____

City: _____

State/Province: _____

Postal/Zip Code: _____ Country: _____

Association for Research and Enlightenment, Inc.
215 67th Street
Virginia Beach, VA 23451-2061

For Faster Service call 1-800-723-1112
www.are-cayce.com

For three days, try the following kind of prayer about that memory. First, say a prayer of thanks for the good that came to you from that situation or relationship. Then, send a blessing to anyone who was involved. Finally, ask for insight about how it prepared you to meet better the opportunities you have right *now* in your life.

Freedom from Possessiveness

Love, in its greatest aspect, does not *possess!* It *is!* It is not then possessive—to be real.   1821-1

$I\!T'\!S$ one of those mysterious paradoxes of life that you can't help but run up against: to grasp means to lose. Whenever you try to possess something, to clutch it tightly, it's sure to slip away. What seems like the most natural response to something desirable—that is, to hold it firmly and own it—backfires. Ironically, it drives away the very person or situation you want so much.

Almost all of us have a story about how we've learned this lesson the hard way. Many have made this painful discovery in a frustrating love relationship, either on the giving or the receiving end of the possessive attitude. If you were the object of someone's attachment and felt his or her possessive clutch, you probably tried to free yourself as soon as you realized what was occurring. Or, if you were the one who felt the compulsion to hold on to someone, you'll remember how terrible it felt to be rebuffed.

Even though we've all heard the theory that possessiveness and genuine love are incompatible—even though we know this from firsthand *experience*—nevertheless, we forget and slip back into it. But oftentimes we make the mistake in little, subtle ways. We may know better than to try to possess another person. What we want instead seems much more modest: that individual's admiration; we want to own that person's esteem. Unfortunately, *any* attempt to be possessive is likely to get the same results—rejection and lack of acceptance.

This is exactly what happened to Paul, a middle-aged salesman whose longtime friend Rachel helped him obtain a reading from Edgar Cayce. Rachel was happily married and her friendship with Paul was clearly a Platonic one. (In fact, her life reading from Cayce said that they had been brother and sister in a previous life and that they still carried that bond.) But Paul coveted her good opinion. He wanted to possess her admiration. So in his reading he asked Cayce about his feelings of inferiority whenever he was around her. The answer was pointed and direct: real love doesn't try to possess anyone or anything. If Rachel's admiration comes of her own free will, then you can gratefully accept it. But it can't be grasped, held, or owned.

Mini-motivator: Stop trying to possess people's esteem. Be yourself and let others be themselves. If someone admires you, enjoy it. But don't grasp for it.

Hopeful Possibilities

For so long as there is life, there is hope. So long as there
is hope, there is possibility. So long as there is possibility,
love may better direct . . .   3647-1

A terse note was lying on her desk when she came into
work that Monday morning. This would be her last week
of work, it coldly announced.

After thirteen years of loyal service, this pink slip was
her fate. The job was a modest one—bookkeeping and
typing—but she had done it with pride and skill. Now
she was being laid off because the company's fortunes
had taken a downward turn. Abigail felt lost. At forty-
eight years of age it hardly seemed possible for her to
start all over again with a new career.

What followed was a period of many months of un-
employment But her search for a new job also became a
search for new meaning in her life. She came across an
article about Edgar Cayce in the popular magazine *Coronet*. It intrigued her so much that she bought a copy of
Cayce's biography *There Is a River* and eventually wrote
to him to request a reading about her career problems.
Her letter to Cayce frankly admitted, "I have reached one
of the darkest places in my life."

It took many months for her to obtain her reading. By

1944 Cayce's notoriety had spread, and he was receiving dozens of requests each week for readings. The wait was difficult for Abigail. She was pinning her hopes on what she'd get in that reading and she was still unemployed.

When the reading finally came, it was very specific and straightforward. You're suited for a new vocational direction, it advised. You're a very talented woman and those talents should be used more directly to serve others. In at least two previous lifetimes you've been skilled in helping others through nursing. Take up that medical career again. Get the training you'll need, and then get on with this deep purpose that lives in your soul.

Those words of advice lifted Abigail's spirits. She had already considered the idea of becoming a nurse but wasn't sure that at her age she'd do very well in the necessary training program. The reading allowed her to see it as a valid possibility. It gave her hope.

In fact, if we look carefully at her entire reading from Cayce it may seem that something was even more important than the specific career recommendation. She was given one of the keys to a life filled with love and fulfillment. The very fact that you are *alive* means that there is *hope*. All you need to do is believe in yourself enough to look for it. When you get in touch with this feeling of hope, then you'll start to see that your life really does have *possibilities*. And with a sense of possibilities, there comes an excitement and a promise that makes *loving* the natural response.

Mini-motivator: Pick a relationship where you'd like to be more loving, even if it sometimes seems hard. Then, for three days try to be more aware of the *possibilities* that exist in that relationship. As you see options, feel how that frees you up to be more optimistic and loving toward that person.

Beyond Barriers

Remember, true love knows not barriers of any kind that
are only of man's creation. For man is the co-creator with
the builder and the maker of the universe . . .   3351-1

If you really are a cocreator with God—as the Cayce
readings and many other sources teach—then what are
you making *this* day? That sort of question might make
you a bit uncomfortable. It's no fun to be put on the spot.
It's sometimes disturbing to look carefully at and recognize the reality you're shaping by your attitudes, feelings,
and purposes.

The answer you might be likely to come up with is
more or less neutral. "In my mental world I'm just re-
hashing my concerns and my plans. It's not really bad,
but I guess it's not that great either."

But Cayce's angle on cocreativity never lets us be on
the fence. There's no middle ground. With each thought,
with each emotion, we're either building up or tearing
down. Or put another way: We're either building

bridges or we're building barriers.

Barriers seemingly get in the way of love. They cut our connections with others, they block the easy flow of energy. So when we run headlong into one of these obstacles, it's natural to want to do something about it. Two immediate options present themselves, both motivated by the desire to be more loving and to heal wounded relationships. But one is more consistent with the highest spiritual law.

Approach One involves taking personal responsibility, saying to yourself, "No doubt, I had some part in the creation of this barrier. So if it was once within my power to make such an obstacle, it's also in my power to unmake it." This method works. It often requires considerable effort, but it's effective. The walls between you and another person may have grown very tall and thick over the years, but the creative power of mind can conquer those barriers.

Approach Two is spiritually wiser. It doesn't deny the truth of personal responsibility and creative mind. However, it operates under a law that is even more potent: Love knows no barrier. In other words, genuine love doesn't have to hassle with the walls. It just goes right on through, as surely as a radio transmission signal passes directly through the walls of your house. Those walls in your house may do a very effective job of resisting the rain, heat, and cold. But they're nothing to the high vibrations of the radio transmission. That signal doesn't "see" the barrier; it doesn't "know" the obstacle.

What's it like to use the second approach? First of all, you stop wrestling with the barriers. Maybe they're there, but you're not going to give them any more power by focusing attention on them. You're not going to give them energy by imagining how you'll scale over them or break through them with the creative power of your mind. Your genuine love for the other person allows you *to see through them.*

Mini-motivator: Imagine today that your love is like a powerful radio transmission of very high frequency. It's going to get through to people. For today you're not going to be limited by any walls. You're not going to be concerned about any barriers. Carry that image—that analogy—in your mind all day long . . . and *act* on it.

The Need to Love

> . . . each soul, each entity, each body, finds the need of expressing that called love in the material experience; from its first awareness until its last call through God's other door . . .   2174-2

WHAT do you need? Not, what do you want, but what do you really *need* in order to be whole and happy?

There's a well-known answer to this question. Dr. Abraham Maslow, one of the founders of humanistic psychology, proposed a hierarchy of human needs. They form a sequence. Theoretically humans have little interest in one level of need unless the lower levels have first been satisfied. Initially come basic physical requirements, such as food and shelter. Next come our fundamental psychological requirements, such as the need to receive love and to have self-esteem. Only higher in the pyramid come needs such as creativity, selfless love, and self-transcendence.

Although Cayce's picture of human needs doesn't directly contradict Maslow's, it does offer a different slant, particularly when it comes to the need to give love. Rather than see it as a higher level that comes only when one is mature, Cayce suggests that something in us *needs to give out love right from childhood.* In other words, the impulse to love is innately a part of being human. It's not something that comes only after life has met certain preconditions for us.

This principle was a central point in Sally's reading which came at a time in her life when she was being forced to look at inner and outer conditions she had avoided for years. For one thing, she was lonely. Some years ago her husband had died. The two of them had run a private school together, and she carried on with her teaching after his death. Although money was no problem—she came from a wealthy family—security in financial matters didn't make up for the lack she felt since his death.

Here was the heart of Cayce's counsel to her: Every soul has a need to express love—at *every* point in one's life span. You can't—and you shouldn't—try to avoid that authentic need. Meeting that need may or may not involve marrying again. Romantic love and the companionship of marriage is only one of many ways in which that need can be addressed.

Just how much are you in touch with that same need of your soul? When you think about what you require in life, is your list made up exclusively of what you must receive? Or have you come to recognize just how vital a need you have to give?

Mini-motivator: The next time you have a day when things don't seem to be going right—a day when something appears to be missing but you don't know what it is—consider the following possibility: The need that's not being met is your need to express love, your need to give. Then, follow up on that possibility. Rearrange your priorities for the day as much as you can and make room for doing something that's motivated strictly by your need to support, help, or care for someone else.

Angels

(Q) *What precautions should be taken to counteract danger periods mentioned?*
(A) . . . *every* individual has what may be *termed* (from the material plane) its own guardian angel, or influence. *Love* and *its* effects guards *this* entity. Depend upon the motive force in love's influence.   2670-3

WHAT images come to your mind with the word "love"? Maybe memories of close connections with friends and family—the best kind of experience that life has to offer. Or perhaps you get images of the overly romanticized version of love that's portrayed in movies, books, and television. But your mixture of pictures, memories, and feelings no doubt revolves around interpersonal relationships.

There's another kind of love that isn't person-to-person. It's the supportive, protective influence that comes from a higher realm. It's hard to describe—hard to get a handle on—simply because it doesn't originate in the familiar, material world. But it's just as real and potent a form of love as the closest person-to-person bond you've ever known.

As a child, you might have been more inclined to notice this sort of love. Do you remember a time when you felt protected or guided, but there wasn't any particular person from which these feelings seemed to be emanating? That loving support was just there. You may have even called it your angel.

As adults we easily dismiss the idea of angelic forces, relegating it to characters like Santa Claus or the Easter bunny—images we're supposed to outgrow by the age of six or seven. To believe in angels seems naive, at best; a ploy to shirk responsibility, at the worst.

Why did the source of the Cayce readings encourage people to be open and sensitive to angels? That kind of advice was given not just to children but to adults—even smart, sophisticated grown-ups. Could it be that angels are one quite authentic way in which we experience universal love?

Could it be that each one of us has his or her own special angel—a being of light that quietly and subtly nudges us in the direction of our spiritual destiny? Maybe that sounds like wishful thinking, something that would be almost too good to be true. But don't you sometimes have inklings of just how true it is?

Contact with your guardian angel doesn't necessarily come as a visual experience, although on rare occasions that can happen. More often the connection comes when one simply feels reassured. Can you recall a time when you suddenly felt strengthened and bolstered as you tried to deal with a challenging situation? Or can you remember being inspired about life, even though there was no good reason to feel that way? Those moments of being touched by universal sources of love—a form of love beyond the personal—might well be described as encounters with your angel.

Mini-motivator: This day be alert—both inwardly and outwardly—for evidence of your angel, an expression of universal love directed toward you individually. Notice moments when your spirits are lifted, even though there may be nothing in the material world around you to cause it. Be receptive to feelings of support and reassurance, even if you can't explain them.

The Human Family

(Q) *What can I contribute to the freedom of India and the brotherhood of man?*
(A) This is a large order, my brother! The brotherhood of man—preach it ever! O, that man would gain the understanding in his heart of this universality of the truth, that man *is* his brother's keeper! 866-1

WE all have days of lofty intentions, days when we get inspired and have a strong feeling that we really could make a difference in the world. Are those moments ones of fanciful ego-inflation? Or are they a glimpse of what really is possible for a single individual? Here's one of the best examples from the Cayce readings of a person determined to make a positive impact.

When Ravi was a young man living in his native India, he studied the religions and philosophies of the world. After reading Emerson, Whitman, and Thoreau, he was inspired to travel to the United States to fulfill what he felt to be his destiny: to become a spiritual teacher.

He arrived in America at the age of twenty, and over the years that followed became more and more well known for his lectures and classes. Upon hearing about Edgar Cayce, he requested a reading in 1935, asking for guidance about his mission. The encouragement Ravi received was a further stimulus to his life's work. While noting that he had launched upon quite a big task— "This is a large order, my brother!" (866-1)—Cayce nevertheless reemphasized just how important this message of universality is to humanity.

Ravi's outreach continued to expand. He authored many books, the last three of which dealt with the teachings of Jesus. In his fifty years of lecturing, he spoke to more than five million people. Even though he lived and worked in the United States, he never forgot his responsibilities to his homeland India. Not only was he an influential advocate of Indian independence from Britain, he also helped many young men and women from India get their education in America. Some of them returned to their homeland and later became members of Parliament, chief ministers in the government, doctors, and scientists.

Admittedly, most of us have not entered this lifetime with a destiny to reach the millions that Ravi did. But we can still carry that same intention and spirit. Cayce's answer to him in 1935 is also a message to each of us today: Live and preach the ideal that we are one human family, that we are brothers and sisters to each other. That kind of experience happens most potently in subtle ways. Principally by our feelings and thoughts about each other we can either help build a universal humanity *or* contribute to the barriers that separate us. The points of division are many: race, nation, gender. But a loving spirit sees through those appearances.

The life story of this remarkable man who was only briefly touched by the Cayce readings can be an inspiration to us. He is an example of one individual who felt deeply and then courageously lived out his life's calling. Each of us also has a mission to create understanding and to promote the oneness of the human family.

Mini-motivator: Work with these attitudes for one day: With each person you encounter, keep in mind the following ideal: "This person before me now is—spiritually speaking—my brother (or my sister)." Let that orientation in your mind direct your words and your deeds.

Overcoming Inner Laziness

Then, do not sit still *and expect the other to do all the giving, nor all the forgiving; but make it rather as the unison and the purpose of each to be that which is a* complement *one to the other, ever.* 939-1

ADAM just wasn't sure. This was a big decision, as big as any he'd ever faced. Although he projected an air of self-assurance and competence in his professional life as a New York City attorney, this was no legal case. There were no law books to tell him what to do in this matter of the heart.

He and Juliet had been dating for six months. Now the time for her leaving was approaching. She had responsibilities and a career of her own to follow elsewhere. Unless there were marriage prospects with Adam, there seemed to be little reason for her to remain in New York.

Adam's friend David Kahn was a longtime friend and supporter of Edgar Cayce. When David learned the details of what Adam and Juliet faced, he suggested they try some advice from a Cayce reading. Together they carefully wrote down the questions they wanted answered and mailed them off to Virginia Beach.

The reading that came back was thrilling to their emotions, but it also contained a sobering challenge to their wills. On the one hand, they were told that marriage to each other had a good chance for success. Their love for each other was genuine.

At the same time, Cayce's counsel focused on a common trait on which they'd have to work. Each had a tendency to let someone else do what needed doing. His advice: Don't sit still and count on your spouse to be the one who does all the giving and the forgiving. In other words, *don't be lazy*. If you want this marriage to work, then you've got to use your will.

The reading went on to cover other topics, but this veiled reference to laziness was probably the most important piece of advice. We tend to think of laziness as a failure to accomplish distasteful tasks, such as lawnmowing or housecleaning. Probably Cayce had this idea in mind because any marriage is likely to be strained if one person does all the labor. But more important, the reading is referring to a kind of *inward laziness*—a willingness or even expectation that the other person will do all the inner work to keep the relationship going. Apparently Adam and Juliet were up for the challenge because soon thereafter they married.

Think about the relationships that *work well* for you, marriage or otherwise. One common feature is simply this: Both of you do your own share of *inner* work—both of you try your best to change biases, let go of a little resentment, and maintain a tolerant attitude. It's inner laziness to presume that the other person should do it all. Authentic loving which leads to lasting relationships requires an act of will to overcome this elusive form of la-

ziness. Mature loving means doing your share, outwardly and inwardly.

Mini-motivator: Pick one relationship where you
know there's a foundation of love, but one in which
things haven't been going very smoothly lately. For three
days make a commitment to overcome any aspect of
your own *inner laziness*. Step up your own internal work
on changing attitudes or feelings that are contributing
to the difficulty.

Attracting Those in Need

> . . . by the beauty of thy purpose, attract others to you, who
> themselves have problems.   5231-1

AMELIA understood the laws of the universe. She was a
serious student of metaphysics and had a profound
knowledge of how the invisible and visible worlds relate.
But in spite of all this learning, something was missing.
She felt as if love had passed her by. Her material life was
full of all that she could want; her head was full. Yet
something in her heart was still empty.

It wasn't surprising that she heard about Edgar Cayce.
Any committed student of metaphysics in the early
1940s was bound to discover this man and his work. So
she eagerly wrote to him in Virginia Beach and requested
a reading. Foremost in her mind was the hope that he
could help her fill this inner vacancy.

The advice that came back to her identified one character trait that often got in her way. Her perceptive nature was quick to notice shortcomings and faults. A
tendency to condemn others for their weaknesses had
to be dealt with and overcome. In order to experience
the unconditional love that she hoped for, she first had
to free herself from this obstacle.

It was hard for her to face up to that trait and admit

how often she was harshly critical. But what made it easier for her to undertake the task of changing was a remarkable promise that Cayce added: Alive within you are beautiful purposes. Others can sense your high ideals and loving intent. They are going to be drawn to you. But those who will come are those who are needy, those who are broken and wounded. You, Amelia, can make a home for other women who have wandered and erred. You can create a place that brings rest, peace, and comfort—a place where people will support and look out for each other. You have the ability to do it. You can "mete to thy fellow . . . sisters in all walks of experience, that love of which ye are capable in thine self." (5231-1)

This image of her destiny and soul's purpose was an inspiration to her. Letting go of her critical nature was made a lot less difficult by having a picture of what was possible. She realized that this empty place in her heart was never going to be filled by studying more books or gaining more in-depth knowledge about herself. Love would come into her life as she joyfully accepted those who would be drawn to her, those who would intuitively sense that she had resources to meet their needs.

It was a bold move for Amelia to take Cayce's words and apply them in her life. The fearful, self-doubting part of her wanted nothing to do with this vision of her mission. That aspect of herself which felt as if love had passed her by didn't want to give; it wanted to get. The last thing in the world it was interested in was a bunch of needy people and their problems.

But love often works just the opposite of the way we expect. Unconditional love operates paradoxically. When we feel as if we're virtually on empty, love allows us to give out to those who have an *even greater* need than our own. In so doing, we are filled.

Mini-motivator: The next time you're feeling short on

love, try a radical approach. If your heart feels rather empty, be willing to give what you've got to someone who is drawn to you with his or her own need or problem. See if you experience an inner filling of your own heart.

Surrendering Privilege

... do not stand too oft upon thy privileges but rather humble thyself that ye may ... bring to the consciousness of others that love that is so near at hand ...   1404-1

ELIZABETH was a remarkable woman in her times. She was born in Texas in 1882, when there were few options for a woman. But going against the expectations and wishes of countless people—family, friends, teachers— she pursued with great determination a career in medicine. Her courageous vision and focused will paid off. She earned her medical degree and began a long, fruitful vocation as a doctor.

When she heard of Edgar Cayce in the mid-1930s she was intrigued. On the one hand, she was fascinated with his abilities to clairvoyantly diagnose illnesses. If he was genuine, she could well imagine her own work being helped by collaboration with someone of his talents. But at the same time, something else about Cayce interested her: a chance to understand *herself* better. So, rather than initially request a reading on one of her patients, she asked for a reading about herself.

Cayce's inner source spoke highly of this accomplished woman, saying even that it was an honor to look deeply into her soul record. In this lifetime of devoted service to the needs of others, she had made a high degree of spiritual development. Yet, since no one is perfect, there was one feature of her personality that needed work. It was the tendency to allow her privileged position in life to stand between her and someone else. Being special could potentially be a block to love.

What a strange notion that seems to be! Don't we try to be special so that others will notice us, admire us, and give us the love we want? Isn't the privilege that comes from accomplishment something for which to strive? Perhaps Cayce's point to Elizabeth—and to all of us— calls for a careful distinction. Yes, we should make the best use of our talents and do all that we can. Setting goals and being successful are part of our spiritual tasks. But then, if we *do* make considerable achievements, we've got to be very careful with the privileges that come with worldly success.

For example, Elizabeth was a highly accomplished professional. Especially in her day, a physician was a powerful authority figure. She was a privileged person because her superior knowledge, reasoning skills, and medical know-how gave her a great degree of respectability. Without denying the positive contributions that she could make in her role as a doctor, she had to remember that *it was only a role.* Like a double-edged sword, it bestowed on her many benefits and advantages. She had to be careful that they never got in the way of authentically meeting someone soul-to-soul. Cayce advised that she work at making sure that privileges—no matter how well deserved—never became a barrier to her ability to love someone.

The same principle holds true for us, no matter what degree of prestige our roles in life may offer. It feels nice to be special and to earn advantages. It's a boost to our self-esteem. Some of the privileges make life a little easier to endure. But at the same time, we need to be wary of holding too tightly to a privileged self-image because it can sometimes become a very resistant barrier to love.

Mini-motivator: Today try to meet other people soul-to-soul. Be willing to let go of any advantaged or privileged position that your role in life gives you, especially if you see that it might be a barrier to love.

Transforming Disappointment

> . . . know the whole truth that makes one free indeed; that
> love that prevents slurs, slights, unkind remarks, falterings
> here, disappointments there . . . few have found this.
>
> 262-44

LOVE is the antidote to many human ills, especially the
ones that crop up in relationships. In those moments
when we've freed ourselves to love unconditionally,
something wonderful happens. Gone is the compulsion
to compete with others. Little remarks that would hurt
someone simply don't come to mind. Disappointments
seem to evaporate.

The link between love and disappointment is particularly important. When you feel let down by someone, it's
hard to maintain a loving attitude. But conversely, when
your heart is filled with love, events or behaviors that
would usually disappoint you seem to have lost their
power.

Edgar Cayce counseled one young woman about this
very point. Hannah was a young stage actress trying to
make her way in New York. Life was tough, but she was
determined to succeed. Continually she had to deal with
disappointment, not only feeling dismayed when rejected at tryouts but also feeling let down by unreliable

people in the business. How was she to cope with this demanding vocational path?

The advice in her reading asked her to think about disappointment and to see it in a new light. There is a way to disarm the negative impact of disappointment, Cayce counseled her. It requires you to be compassionate, to be more empathetically connected to people around you. "But weep with those who weep and rejoice with those who do rejoice, in the Lord! These will make for the non-effect of the disappointments . . . " (1129-2)

This isn't a formula on avoiding disappointment. It's a method for transforming the negative effect that's so common. When we're disappointed, the tendency is to withdraw into ourselves. For a while we cut ourselves off from the world with self-pity. But Cayce taught Hannah another approach to use in those moments that would invariably arise in her career: When you're let down and saddened, let it make you sensitive to other people who are going through the same sort of experience.

Sure, it's more fun to rejoice with those who rejoice. But just as authentically we can feel our connections with others—that is, our love for them—by compassionately feeling sadness as they do. In fact, this very formula is the way the Cayce readings described how Jesus lived His life. He wept with those who wept, and He rejoiced with those who rejoiced.

None of this means that we should seek disappointment so that we can feel connected to others out of empathetic love. Life will bring us plenty of opportunities without our having to go looking for them. But this principle from Cayce's psychology of love is a valuable new angle on a frequent challenge. Maybe disappointment isn't necessarily the mirror opposite of love and is always canceling it out. If we look with a fresh perspective, we may see that disappointment can become a stepping-stone to feeling closer to others. We can transform the *effect* of disappointment by following Jesus' example.

Mini-motivator: The next time you feel disappointed resist the temptation to cut yourself off from the world with self-pity. Use the disappointment as a way to make you more sensitive and loving. Be willing to feel your own hurt or sadness, and then let it make you more empathetically aware of the same feelings that may be going on within others.

Healing Love

> . . . love thy neighbor as thyself. This brings into the consciousness that peace which each soul seeks, and brings with same healing . . .   1747-5

EDGAR Cayce was first and foremost a healer. This was how he understood his life's work. Although he lacked training in medical techniques, his career focused on easing the pain of those who suffered. But from where did this extraordinary ability to diagnose baffling illnesses originate? How could a man whose formal education ended with eighth grade be so wise—so medically savvy—as an adult?

One biographer, Dr. Harmon Bro, who watched and worked with Cayce firsthand, has characterized his life as "love surprised by wisdom." In other words, here was a man who genuinely loved people, and out of that love an unexpected byproduct emerged: remarkable wisdom for healing.

One has only to study Cayce's correspondence with his friends and clients to see evidence of that loving concern. His time was in constant demand, yet he regularly wrote lengthy letters to those who were trying to understand their readings. Those who requested and paid for his services weren't consumers to him; they were people who had become his friends.

This view of his life runs counter to the common perception of Cayce as the amazing psychic, the doer of miracles. No doubt he *was* gifted with clairvoyant abilities; no doubt miracles *did* occur in the lives of many individuals. But it misses the point to depict the man as fundamentally a performer of dazzling mental tricks. It distorts the example that his life could be for us today. Time and again, the information that came through Edgar Cayce reminded us that *we are all meant to be healers.*

How do we claim our own healing ministry? How do we unlock our own, unique healing talents? For most of us it won't involve becoming a physician or a psychic reader. More likely we'll be called upon to help heal wounds that cause mental, emotional, or spiritual pain. We'll be given the opportunity to support, encourage, and believe in people. The best way to discover our own healing skill is to follow Cayce's example: start with love and then be surprised by what comes.

It takes courage to follow that formula. Too often we want to know in advance how a problem will get solved. It's often hard simply to start by loving and then to trust. Suppose, for example, that a work colleague has become dispirited about her job and feels boxed in. Can you be a healer in that situation? Maybe you don't have vocational counseling skills. Maybe you don't have the ready-made solution to her depression. But you *can* start with loving her, being willing to listen and to be supportive. What's likely to follow may surprise you both. Perhaps something you say will trigger a new idea for her. Perhaps your genuine show of concern will lift her self-esteem. You will have been a healer for her, and it will have been simply a byproduct of your love.

Mini-motivator: Spend today thinking of yourself as a

healer. Rather than hurry through your interactions with other people, take time to listen and show your concern. Let yourself be surprised by what comes from you out of that basic love for people.

About the Author

Mark Thurston, Ph.D., is an educator, psychologist, and author of more books on the Cayce readings than any other writer. His sixteen books cover virtually all the aspects of Cayce's approach to spiritual disciplines, soul growth, human relations, and how we creatively shape the future. He has played leadership roles with both the Association for Research and Enlightenment, Inc., (A.R.E.) and Atlantic University in his more than twenty-five years with these organizations.

Among his most significant previous publications are two books about dream interpretation—*Dreams: Tonight's Answers for Tomorrow's Questions* and *How to Interpret Your Dreams.* He is also widely known for his workshops, training courses, and books on the subject of finding one's mission in life, including *Discovering Your Soul's Purpose* and *Soul-Purpose: Discovering and Fulfilling Your Destiny.*

He is a regular contributor to *Venture Inward* magazine, and his columns have been compiled in two books—*The Great Teachings of Edgar Cayce* and *More Great Teachings of Edgar Cayce.*

In addition to writing, Dr. Thurston was executive producer and host for a twenty-six-part television series, *The New Millennium,* which was produced at WHRO, the Norfolk/Virginia Beach PBS affiliate. It has aired nationally on The Wisdom Network.

Dr. Thurston has been married for twenty years to Mary Elizabeth Lynch, a practicing attorney and mediator. They work and reside in Virginia Beach, Virginia, with their two children.

A.R.E. PRESS

The A.R.E. Press publishes quality books, videos, and audiotapes meant to improve the quality of our readers' lives—personally, professionally, and spiritually. We hope our products support your endeavors to realize your career potential, to enhance your relationships, to improve your health, and to encourage you to make the changes necessary to live a loving, joyful, and fulfilling life.

For more information or to receive a free catalog, call

1-800-723-1112

Or write

A.R.E. Press
215 67th Street
Virginia Beach, VA 23451-2061

DISCOVER HOW THE EDGAR CAYCE MATERIAL CAN HELP YOU!

The Association for Research and Enlightenment, Inc. (A.R.E.®), was founded in 1931 by Edgar Cayce. Its international headquarters are in Virginia Beach, Virginia, where thousands of visitors come year-round. Many more are helped and inspired by A.R.E.'s local activities in their own hometowns or by contact via mail (and now the Internet!) with A.R.E. headquarters.

People from all walks of life, all around the world, have discovered meaningful and life-transforming insights in the A.R.E. programs and materials, which focus on such areas as holistic health, dreams, family life, finding your best vocation, reincarnation, ESP, meditation, personal spirituality, and soul growth in small-group settings. Call us today on our toll-free number

1-800-333-4499

or

Explore our electronic visitor's center on the
Internet: **http://www.edgarcayce.org.**

We'll be happy to tell you more about how the work of the A.R.E. can help you!

A.R.E.
215 67th Street
Virginia Beach, VA 23451-2061